Neil Simon Scenes

NEIL SIMON SCENES

Scenes from the Works of America's Foremost Playwright

Edited by Roger Karshner

ACTING EDITION

Dramaline® Publications

Dramaline Publications, 36-851 Palm View Road
Rancho Mirage, CA 92270
Phone: 619/770-6076 Fax: 619/770-4507
E-mail: drama.line@gte.net Web: www.dramaline.com

Library of Congress Cataloging-in-Publication-Data

Simon, Neil.
   [Selections. 2000]
   Neil Simon scenes : scenes from the works of America's foremost playwright / edited by Rogr Karshner. — Acting ed.
      p. cm.
   ISBN 0-949669-48-X (alk. paper)
   1. Acting—Auditions. I. Karshner, Roger. II. Title.
PS3537.1663 A6 2000
812'. 54—dc21   00-046787

Cover art by John Sabel

This book is printed on paper that meets the requirements of the American Standard of Permanence of paper for printed library material.

CONTENTS

FOREWORD

Neil Simon is the only writer, no, the only person that I have never heard speaking the words, "It would be funny if he (she) said it right." To the contrary. Back when we first started doing plays together, him writing, me directing, it always took every ounce of persuasion that I could muster to keep him from rewriting the whole play after every reading, every rehearsal. I would beg for a little time. I would say the actors need a day or two to get the rhythms, I need a day or two to stage it. Doc would say, "No, no, the actors are fine, you're fine, I can just make it better."

Sometimes I was able to stop him for a day or two. Sometimes I wasn't. When we were out of town with *The Odd Couple* he brought in a rewrite that contained, among other things, Oscar saying "You write me little notes: 'We are all out of milk. F.U.' It took me twenty minutes to figure out that F.U. meant Felix Unger." We thought nothing of it and put the line in the play. That night when Walter Matthau said it the laugh was so long that he had to sit down and read an entire issue of the *N.Y Post* to fill up time during it.

We had so many different endings to *The Odd Couple* that to this day I can't remember how it ends except that it ends well.

I remember those days the way we are meant to remember our childhoods and rarely can. We were really happy. Neil was a very great comedy writer finding his excitement and discovering where it led him and those of us who did his plays were astonished and excited too. I remember often standing in the back and one of us saying, "We have to kill that laugh somehow if the scene is going to work." It was impossible to keep the audience from laughing.

We were laughing too because we were having such a good time. I don't mean we chuckled over cocktails all the time. It was hard work sometimes and we never stopped improving it, we went out of town for long times and worked and worked. But we were happy because it was so damn funny and also good. The audience was always way ahead of us in pleasure. They always liked it much better than we did as we polished and improved.

(*next page*)

(*continued*)

From that day on it has always seemed to me the ideal situation that the audience should like it more than you do while you are working on a play. The people working on it should first look to themselves to improve it, not to the others.

All this comes from Neil. He is never satisfied, always working on how it can be better. I don't see how he could be better. I loved him then and I love him now. He stands alone in his category, he is the standard, but he will never be alone because of all of us who love him.

MIKE NICHOLS
NEW YORK, NEW YORK

INTRODUCTION

This book offers actors a wide range of scenes that are intended for workshop, audition and classroom use only. Attention should be given to the terms of copyright with specific attention to public performance.

The synopses of the plays cover major plot points and offer a general story outline. They will never, however, compensate for reading and studying the play scripts and viewing videos of the plays that have been brought to film (plays on video and laser are identified with a V or L or both under the title). In order for you to fully understand your character's relationship to the piece, it is strongly suggested that you thoroughly familiarize yourself with the playscript. All plays are published by Samuel French, Inc., with the exception of *The Star-Spangled Girl,* which is published by Dramatists Play Service

Editing these plays has been a rewarding experience because it has given me the opportunity of becoming intimate with their characters—funny, sad, tragic and endearing. I have been able to climb into their skin for a few moments and view the world from their perspective. It has been a rewarding journey. I trust that you will travel this same enriching road as you bring voice to Mr. Simon's people.

ROGER KARSHNER
RANCHO MIRAGE, CALIFORNIA

COME BLOW YOUR HORN

Premièred February 22, 1961
at the Brooks Atkinson Theatre, New York City

Directed by Stanley Prager

CAST

Alan Baker	Hal March
Peggy Evans	Arlene Golonka
Buddy Baker	Warren Berlinger
Mr. Baker	Lou Jacobi
Connie Dayton	Sarah Marshall
Mrs. Baker	Pert Kelton
A Visitor	Carolyn Brenner

The action of the play takes place in Alan's New York apartment.

Harry Baker is the proprietor of a waxed-fruit business and his two sons are in his employ: Alan, a profligate, malingerer and womanizer; and Buddy, a dutiful, naive twenty-one-year-old who is still living at home. But Buddy is feeling the constraints of family ties and has decided to declare his independence. So he moves into Alan's bachelor apartment. Alan, more diligent in the pursuit of the good life than the waxed-fruit business, has jeopardized the Meltzer account. When his father demands that he regain the account "or else," Alan sets up a swinging party with Meltzer that backfires when their mother intervenes. Buddy's departure ruptures his relationship with his father, and Alan's blowing the Meltzer account results in his termination. So the two sons, or "bums" as their father calls them, are now on their own, disowned by their father.

Alan, distressed by being ostracized and unable to make an honest emotional commitment to his girlfriend, Connie, becomes more and more serious, but Buddy, thanks to lessons in "living" from the worldly Alan, becomes a self-confident swinger. This role reversal strains their relationship and leads to minor conflict. Then, Mother arrives with her suitcase, announcing that she can no longer tolerate her husband's intractability toward his sons. A final scene involving Alan, Buddy, Mother, Father, and Connie leads to understanding and resolution: Alan is marrying Connie and returning to the business, Mother and Father are off on a trip around the world. And Buddy? Buddy will be back marketing waxed fruit, too. He will also be living independently, pursuing the "good life."

From Act I:
Alan—25-35
Peggy—20-30

Alan and Peggy have just returned to his bachelor apartment from a weekend at a ski resort where Alan told her he was taking her to meet Mr. Manheim, a film executive. Peggy, a lovely young woman whose I. Q. matches her waistline, is poured into a ski outfit exposing every curve and crevice. Overcoming her feeble protestations, Alan, the ultimate seducer, has the gullible Peggy in his apartment and out of her jacket in no time—the naive girl is no match for this charming manipulator.

When Peggy quizzes Alan regarding Mr. Manheim (there was never a Mr. Manheim), he artfully answers her questions with fractured logic. Near the end of the scene, Alan refers to Peggy as

Connie, a woman who has had an unsettling emotional impact upon this normally love-insulated roué. The scene is interrupted by the arrival of Alan's younger brother, Buddy.

PEGGY. Alan, No!

ALAN. Come on, honey.

PEGGY. Alan, no.

ALAN. (*Taking off her ski jacket. Places it on luggage.*) Just five more minutes. Come on.

PEGGY. Alan, no, Please. (*He pulls her into the living room.*)

ALAN. But you said you were cold.

PEGGY. I am.

ALAN. (*Embracing her.*) I'll start a fire. I'll have your blood going up and down in no time.

PEGGY. Alan, I want to go upstairs and take a bath. I've got about an inch of the New York Thruway on me.

ALAN. Hey, you can't go yet. We've got to have one last drink. To cap the perfect weekend.

PEGGY. It was four days.

ALAN. It's not polite to count—Don't you ever get tired of looking sensational?

PEGGY. Do you think I do?

ALAN. You just saw what happened at the ski jump. They were looking at you and jumping into the parking lot—Come here. (*He bites her on the neck.*)

PEGGY. (*Giggles.*) Why do you always do that?

ALAN. Do what?

PEGGY. Bite me on the neck.

ALAN. What's the matter. You don't think I'm a vampire, do you?

PEGGY. Gee, I never thought of that.

ALAN. If it'll make you feel safer, I'll chew on your ear lobe. (*He does.*)

PEGGY. (*Giggles.*) Kiss me.

ALAN. I'm not through with the hors d'oeuvres yet. (*Nibbles—than he kisses her.*)

PEGGY. (*Sighs and sits on sofa.*) Now I feel warm again.

ALAN. Good.

PEGGY. Thank you for the weekend, Alan. I had a wonderful time.

ALAN. Yeah, it was fun. (*Crossing toward bar.*)

PEGGY. Even though he didn't show up.

ALAN. (*Stops and turns.*) Who?

PEGGY. Your friend from M. G. M.

ALAN. (*Continuing to bar. Quickly.*) Oh, Mr. Manheim. Yeah—Well, that's show biz.

PEGGY. Did it say when he expects to be in New York again?

ALAN. Did what? (*Picks up carton containing Scotch bottle.*)

PEGGY. The telegram. From Hollywood.

ALAN. (*Crosses.*) Oh! Didn't I tell you? Next week. Early part.

PEGGY. It's kind of funny now that you think of it, isn't it?

ALAN. What is?

PEGGY. Him wanting to meet me in a hotel.

ALAN. (*Taking bottle out of carton.*) It was a ski lodge.

PEGGY. Was it? Anyway, it was nice. I've never been to New Hampshire before.

ALAN. It was Vermont. (*Putting down carton on side-board.*)

PEGGY. Oh. I'm terrible with names. I can't imagine why an important man like that wants to travel all the way up there just to meet me.

ALAN. (*Puts bottle on back of bar. Crosses above R. to sofa..*) I explained all that. Since the picture he's planning is all about a winter carnival, he figured the best place to meet you would be against the natural setting of the picture. To see how you photographed against the snow. That makes sense— (*Not too sure.*) Doesn't it? (*Crosses R.*)

PEGGY. Oh, sure.

ALAN. Sure. (*Pulls* Peggy *up from the couch and embraces her.*)

PEGGY. We ought to go up again sometime when it's not for business. Just for fun.

ALAN. *That* should be next week.

PEGGY. Maybe next time I could learn to ski.

ALAN. I wouldn't be surprised.

PEGGY. It's a shame we were cooped up in the room so long.

ALAN. Yes. Well, I explained, we had that bad break in the weather.

PEGGY. You mean all that snow.

ALAN. Exactly—But you make the cutest little Saint Bernard— (*He is just about to kiss her when the BUZZER rings.*)

PEGGY. That's the lobby,

ALAN. I don't hear a thing.

PEGGY. Maybe it's for me.

ALAN. *My* buzzer? You live up in the penthouse.

PEGGY. I know. But I'm always here. (*He looks at her quizzically, then, crossing U. L. C., goes to the wall phone and pick it up.* PEGGY *turns U. R. C., fixing hair.*)

ALAN. (*Into the phone.*) Yes?—Who?—Buddy?—Hi, kid—Now? (*Looks at* Peggy.) Well, sure, if it's important. You know the apartment. (*He hangs up.*) My kid brother. (*Crosses to her.*)

PEGGY. Oh. I'd better go.

ALAN. (*He reaches for her again.*) This is the seventh floor. We still have over a minute.

PEGGY. (*Eluding him, crosses Upstage to foyer. He follows. At R. rail.*) I want to go up and change, anyway. (*She picks up her parka and goes to him, then says invitingly.*) You think he'll be here long?

ALAN. Not when you ask me like that.

PEGGY. Why don't you come up in twenty minutes?

ALAN. Why don't you come down in nineteen?

PEGGY. All right. 'Bye, Alan.

ALAN. (*Starts to embrace her.*) 'Bye, Connie.

PEGGY. Peggy! (*She breaks from him.*)

ALAN. What?

PEGGY. Peggy! That's the third time this weekend you called me Connie.

ALAN. I didn't say Connie. I said, Honey!

PEGGY. Oh!

ALAN. Oh!

PEGGY. Sorry.

(Alan *opens door. She smiles and exits. He closes door* Alan *breathes a sigh of relief. Picks up suitcase and goes into bedroom U. L. as the DOORBELL rings.*)

From Act I:
Alan—25-35
Father—50-60

Alan's younger brother, Buddy, has left home and come to Alan's apartment, packed and ready to move in. Alan welcomes him warmly, supporting his decision to "break out of prison." Near the end of his scene with Buddy, Alan's doorbell sounds. Alan is expecting Peggy's return, but a startling reversal occurs—Alan's father makes an unexpected appearance.

Buddy ducks quietly into the bedroom. Father steps in and looks at Alan and nods disgustingly. Alan looks after him dismayed, and seems puzzled when he doesn't see Buddy. The Father examines the room. It is obvious he approves of nothing in the apartment.

Alan's weekend ski foray with lovely Peggy has resulted in him lousing up the Meltzer account. Mr. Baker, irate, fed up, expresses his displeasure in caustic terms, often referring to his profligate, malingering son as "bum." He berates Alan, ending their scene with an ultimatum: Regain Meltzer's waxed-fruit business, or else!

ALAN. Gee, Dad—this is a—pleasant —surprise. (*The* Father *looks at him as if to say* "I'll bet")

FATHER. How am I?—I'll tell you sometime.—That's how I am. (*He continues his inspection. Crosses L. of* Alan *to coffee table.*)

ALAN. I've redecorated the place—How do you like it?

FATHER. Fancy—Very fancy—You must have some nice job. (*Sniffs a highball glass.*)

ALAN. I just got in, Dad. I was about to call you.

FATHER. The phone company shouldn't have to depend on your business.

ALAN. I wanted to explain what happened to me. Why I wasn't in the last two days.

FATHER. (*Crosses R. a step.*) There's nothing to explain.

ALAN. Yes, there is, Dad.

FATHER. Why? I understand. You work very hard two days a week and you need a five day weekend. That's normal.

ALAN. Dad, I'm not going to lie. I was up in Vermont skiing. I intended to be back Sunday night, but I twisted my bad ankle again. I couldn't drive. I thought it was broken.

FATHER. I'll send you a get-well card.

ALAN. I'm sorry, Dad, I really am.

FATHER. You're sorry. I can't ask for more than that.

ALAN. I'll be in the office first thing in the morning.

FATHER. That's good news. You know the address, don't you?

ALAN. Yes, Dad, I know the address.

FATHER. See. I always knew your were smart. So I'll see you in the morning.

ALAN. Right! (*He starts upstage.*)

FATHER. Oh, by the way—How's the Meltzer account going?

ALAN. The Meltzer account? (*He comes back R. of him.*)

FATHER. From Atlantic City? The one you bragged about was all wrapped up?

ALAN. Oh-er-fine.

FATHER. Fine? I'm glad to hear that—Because he called today.

ALAN. (*Surprised.*) Oh? About an order?

FATHER. Yes. About an order.

ALAN. (*A little skeptical.*) Did—did we get one?

FATHER. Yes—we got one.

ALAN. How much?

FATHER. How much? Guess.

ALAN. Well, Dad, I—

FATHER. Guess! Guess how much we got from Meltzer.

ALAN. Nothing?

FATHER. Bingo! Right on the button! Bum! (*Points to him sharply.*)

ALAN. Dad, wait a minute—

FATHER. (*Crossing to him. Each "Bum" is a sharp point.*) Did you have a nice weekend, bum? Do you know what it costs for skiing for four days? Three thousand dollars a day? Bum!

ALAN. I tried to call him. I couldn't get a line through.

FATHER. On skis you tried to call him? You should be in the Olympics.

ALAN. (*Crossing L. to phone.*) I'll call him right back. I'll explain everything. (*Sits on sofa an picks up phone.*)

FATHER. (*Turns.*) Where you gonna call him?

ALAN. In Atlantic City.

FATHER. Who're you going to talk to? The Boardwalk? He's here!

ALAN. In New York?

FATHER. In the Hotel Croyden. For two days he's sitting waiting while you're playing in the snow. (*Intimates playing, a step D. R.*)

ALAN. (*Hangs up phone, crosses R. to* Father.) Dad, I promise you. I won't lose the account!

FATHER. Why? This would be the first one you ever lost? You want to see the list. You could ski—(*Gestures.*) down your cancellations.

ALAN. I couldn't get back in time, Dad. Skiing had nothing to do with it.

FATHER. (*Crossing D. L. to sofa.*) I'm sorry. I forgot. I left out golf and sailing and sleeping and drinking and women. You're terrific. (*Turns to him.*) If I was in the bum business I would want ten like you.

ALAN. (*Steps L. to C.*) That's not true, I put in plenty of time in the business.

FATHER. (*A step R.*) Two years. In six years you put in two years. I had my bookkeeper figure it out.

ALAN. Thank you.

FATHER. (*Looks at him, turns.*) My own son. I get more help from my competitors. (*Starts to sit R. end of sofa.*)

ALAN. Well, why not? You treat me like one.

FATHER. (*Jumping up, crosses R. to C.*) *I* treat you? Do *I* wander in at eleven o'clock in the morning? Do *I* take three hours for lunch—in night clubs? When are you there? (*Crosses R. to him.*)

ALAN. What do you mean, when?

FATHER. (*Backs L. to C.*) When? When? You take off legal holidays, Jewish holidays, Catholic holidays. Last year you took off Halloween.

ALAN. I was sick.

FATHER. (*Turns R.*) When you came back to work you were sick. When you were sick you were dancing. (*Turns L., imitating dancing.*)

ALAN. (*Crosses L. to him.*) In the first place, it's not true. And in the second place what good does it do coming in? You don't need me. You never ask my advice about the business, do you?

FATHER. What does a skier know about waxed fruit?

ALAN. (*Crosses away R. C.*) You see. You see. You won't even listen.

FATHER. (*He sits on sofa, R. end.*) Come in early. I'll listen.

ALAN. (*Crosses L. to him.*) I did. For three years. Only then I was "too young" to have anything to say. An now that I've got my own apartment, I'm too much of a "bum" to have anything to say. Admit it, Dad. You don't give me the same respect you give the night watchman.

FATHER. At least I know where he is at nights.

ALAN. You know where I am, too. Having fun. What's wrong with it. I think what I do at night should be my business.

FATHER. Not when it's nighttime four days in a row. Listen, what do I care. (*He rises and crosses R. of Alan to D. R. C. chair.*) Do whatever you want. Go ahead and live lie a bum.

ALAN. Why am I a bum?

FATHER. Are you married?

ALAN. No.

FATHER. Then you're a bum!

ALAN. Give me a chance. I'll get married.

FATHER. (*Crossing L. to him.*) I heard that for years. When you were 26, 27, 28, even 29, you were a bachelor. But now you're over thirty and you're still not married, so you're a bum and that's all there is to it. (*Turns away R.*)

ALAN. You made thirty the closing date? All I want to do is have a little fun out of life like any other healthy, normal American boy.

FATHER. (*Turns to him.*) Healthy you are, American you are, normal you're not.

ALAN. What do you mean?

FATHER. Look at your brother, that's what I mean. That's normal. He'll be something, that kid. He'll never be like you. Not in a million years.

ALAN. (*Crosses U.*) Really? He might surprise you.

FATHER. (*Crosses D. R.*) That I'll bet my life on. He's in the plant first thing in the morning, he puts in a whole day's work. No, that's the son I'll never have to worry about! (*Front.*)

ALAN. Have you read your mail lately?

FATHER. (*Turns.*) What?

ALAN. Nothing.

FATHER. (*Crosses U. to R. end of foyer steps, not on.*) All right, I don't want to discuss anything more. I want to see you in the office tomorrow morning at eight o'clock.

ALAN. (*Crosses U. to L. of him.*) Eight o'clock? There's no one there then.

FATHER. You'll be there. And you'll be there two nights a week and Saturday's, holidays, birthdays and vacations. I'm sick and tired of being the father. From now on I'm the boss.

ALAN. All right, Dad, but eight o'clock is silly. I have nothing to do until nine.

FATHER. You play solitaire all day, anyway. You can get in three more games. (*Crossing up to foyer.*)

ALAN. Okay. Okay. I'll be there

FATHER. (*Turns and points.*) With the Meltzer account. If you haven't got it signed and in your pocket—you can ski— (*Gesturing.*) right into the unemployment office.

ALAN. I'll try, Dad. I'll really do my best.

FATHER. With your best, we're in trouble. From you I need a miracle. (*Alan* sits D. R. C. chair.) Eight o'clock with the Meltzer account— (*Crosses to door.*)

ALAN. Yes, Dad.

FATHER. (*Turns.*) The day your brother becomes like you, I throw myself in front of an airplane. (*And with that he exits.*)

From Act II:
Connie and Allen—25-35

Although he has deep feelings for Connie, Alan, the consummate roué, cannot make a commitment. In a previous scene, Connie, openly in love with Alan, offered herself as either a wife or live-in, putting the equivocating Alan in a position of ultimate decision. When he called her bluff by choosing the bedroom, Connie upped the ante by leaving for her "merchandise."

In this scene Connie has returned, suitcase in hand, prepared to be accepted on any terms. But even though Alan loves her, he cannot overcome his penchant for lack of emotional commitment. Disgusted, fed up, Connie leaves the vacillating bachelor in a state of confused apprehension.

(DOORBELL *rings again.* Buddy *exits through the kitchen R.* Alan *opens door,* Connie *stands there with her valise.*)

ALAN. Connie! (*Closes door. She puts down case and gives* Alan *a long kiss interrupting his "Wha—," then when she releases him.*)
CONNIE. Me no Connie. Me Jane. You Tarzan. Jane come to swing with Tarzan in tree.
ALAN. What's in that suitcase?
CONNIE. The rest of my merchandise. (*She takes off her coat. Puts it on R. hand-rail with purse.*)
ALAN. Are you drunk?
CONNIE. On one martini?
ALAN. (*Crossing away R. above R. C. chair.*) You get loaded just ordering one.
CONNIE. Now, then, the bedroom. It's in that direction, isn't it? (*She picks up suitcase and starts for bedroom.*)
ALAN. You stay out of there. What's come over you?

CONNIE. Nothing, darling. I gave you a choice and you made it.

ALAN. What?

CONNIE. Wonderful service, Isn't it? You don't even have to pick it up. We deliver.

ALAN. You're not drunk. You're crazy.

CONNIE. (*Puts down suitcase and crosses R., stalking him as he backs away R.*) Just think of it, darling! We're going to live together, love together. Fun, fun, fun. Sin, sin, sin.

ALAN. (*At R. counter.*) Connie, you're scaring the hell outta me.

CONNIE. (*L. of him.*) You don't even have to say you love me. And when you get bored, just kick me out and give me a letter of recommendation.

ALAN. Will you cut it out? It's not funny any more. (*Backs away L.*)

CONNIE. I don't understand, Alan. Isn't this what you want? Isn't this what you asked for?

ALAN. No.

CONNIE. No.

ALAN. (*L. of C.*) That's right, no. I said I could see nothing wrong for two young people who were very fond of each other to have a healthy, normal relationship. But I see no reason to turn this affair into a—foreign art movie.

CONNIE. Good heavens, sir. I must be in the wrong apartment.

ALAN. Look, I told you before. I'm not denying anything. Six nights a week I'm Leonard Lover. But with you—well, it's different.

CONNIE. (*A step L. to R. C. chair.*) Careful, Alan. You're on the brink of committing yourself.

ALAN. Who's keeping it a secret? I love you.

CONNIE. You weren't very sure.

ALAN. I am now. If I can turn down an offer like this with a girl like you, I must be in love.

CONNIE. Well, then—where does that leave us?

ALAN. (*Turns front.*) I don't know.

CONNIE. (*Sits R. arm of R. C. chair.*) You don't know?

ALAN. (*Crossing to her.*) Look, honey, you've got to give me a chance to think. A lot of things have happened tonight. I just lost my job.

CONNIE. I thought you worked for your father.

ALAN. We must be in a hell of a recession. He just let me go—Oh, Connie, don't you see—

CONNIE. No, I don't see. You love me but you won't marry me, and you love me too much to live with me.

ALAN. (*Crosses around chair to R. of it.*) I know. I can't figure it out either.

CONNIE. (*Angry.*) I see. Well, I'm sorry, Alan, but I can't spend the rest of my life waiting in the hallway. (*She gets up and crosses to C.*)

ALAN. Wait a minute.

CONNIE. (*Turns C.*) For what? I either come in or I go out. You want me or you don't. Yes or no.

ALAN. Why can't things be like they were before?

CONNIE. It's too late. We've raised the stakes.

ALAN. Who made you the dealer all of a sudden?

CONNIE. If the game is too big, Alan, get out.

ALAN. I see. A brilliant maneuver, General. You've got me cornered. Very well, I surrender.

CONNIE. I don't take prisoners. (*She goes to foyer, gets purse.*)

ALAN. (*Crosses to R. end steps; angry.*) I mean it. If that's what you want, I'll marry you.

CONNIE. (*Gets coat. Puts over L. arm.*) If that's the way you'll marry me, I don't want it.

ALAN. (*Crossing to her.*) Connie, wait. Where are you going?

CONNIE. (*Putting on coat.*) Right now I want to be about a thirty-five dollar taxi ride away from you.

ALAN. (*Sincerely. Crossing to her.*) Connie, wait—I don't want you to leave.

CONNIE. (*She's made up her mind.*) I'm sorry.

ALAN. You mean I won't see you again?

CONNIE. I don't know. Maybe if I get lonely enough. (*The* Phone *rings.*) You probably won't have much chance tonight. Start in the morning. (Phone *rings again.* Connie *picks up suitcase.*)

ALAN. Connie, wait.

CONNIE. Answer your phone, Alan. It's the second platoon. (Phone *rings again.*)

ALAN. (*Crosses D. L. C.; picks up phone.*) Hello—Oh, Mom. (*To* CONNIE.) Connie, it's my mother.

CONNIE. Your mother? Oh, come on, Alan. (*She opens door.*)

ALAN. Why should I kid about a thing like that?

CONNIE. Good-bye. (*And she's gone, closing the door behind her.*)

ALAN. Connie— Connie, wait. (*Back into phone. He sits.*) Hello, Mom?— What's wrong? Did Dad get home yet?— Aunt Gussie?— Well, don't worry about it. He'll probably just sleep there tonight. He'll be home tomorrow when he calms down— Mom, please don't cry . . . All right, look, I'll come up and sleep there tonight— Yes, in my old room— I don't feel like being alone either— What?— No, not yet— Mom, please, I'm very upset— I've got a lot on my mind— I can't decide that now— Mom, I don't care—lamb chops, turkey, chicken salad, anything.—

THE ODD COUPLE

(L)

Premièred March 10, 1965
at the Plymouth Theatre, New York City

Directed by Mike Nichols

CAST

Speed	Paul Dooley
Murray	Nathaniel Frey
Roy	Sidney Armus
Vinnie	John Fiedler
Oscar Madison	Walter Matthau
Felix Ungar	Art Carney
Gwendolyn Pigeon	Carole Shelley
Cecily Pigeon	Monica Evans

The action of the play takes place in an apartment on Riverside Drive in New York City.

Oscar Madison, a sports writer, is divorced from his wife Blanche and lives a life of poker and cigars in an apartment in New York City. He is undependable, unreliable, irresponsible, and one of the world's biggest slobs. During one of his traditional Friday night poker parties, Felix Ungar, a writer for CBS news, arrives in a near suicidal state because his wife Frances has given him the boot—she has finally tired of his obsessive neatness and hypochondria.. Oscar invites Felix to move in, a plan doomed from the onset due to their disparate personalities.

Felix transforms the apartment from utter chaos to ordered sterility, applying his gourmet cooking and meticulousness to a degree that drives Oscar up the wall. It's an impossible, oil-and-water situation fomenting endless conflicts and a hilarious situation. As the plot unfolds, the flaws that destroyed their own marriages become manifest in the behavior of the two men, and in a classic example of transference, each take on characteristics of Frances and Blanche.

The play climaxes with an inevitable acrimonious exchange, and Felix moves out. But the dissolution is positive because both he and Oscar have grown and gained insight through their "marital" experience.

From Act I, scene i:
Oscar and Felix—40-50

Oscar's Friday night poker game has disbanded early. Once a raucous, free-wheeling affair of cigarettes, cigars and booze, it is now a sterile nightmare due to Felix's obsessive neatness. After the gang has departed, Oscar takes Felix to task for his penchant for extreme cleanliness, heightened sense of guilt, and hypochondria. He is also fed up with their boring life style and proposes and evening of feminine companionship.

FELIX. (*Staring at door.*) That's funny, isn't it, Oscar? . . . They think we're happy . . . They really think we're enjoying this . . . (*Gets up an begins to straighten up chairs.*) They don't know, Oscar. They don't know what it's like. (*He gives a short, ironic laugh, tucks napkin under arm and starts to pick up dishes from table.*)

OSCAR. I'd be immensely grateful to you, Felix, if you didn't clean up just now.

FELIX. (*Puts dishes on tray.*) It's only a few things . . . (*He stops and looks back at door.*) I can't get over what Murray just said . . . You know I think they really envy us. (*Clears more stuff from table.*)

OSCAR. Felix, leave everything alone. I'm not through dirtying up for the night. (*Drops poker chips on floor.*)

FELIX. (*Putting stuff on tray.*) But don't you see the irony of it? . . . Don't you see it, Oscar?

OSCAR. (*Sighs heavily.*) Yes, I see it.

FELIX. (*Clearing table.*) No, you don't. I really don't think you do.

OSCAR. Felix, I'm telling you I see the irony of it.

FELIX. (*Pauses.*) Then tell me. What is it? What's the irony?

OSCAR. (*Deep breath.*) The irony is—unless we can come to some other arrangement, I'm gonna kill you! . . . That's the irony.

FELIX. What's wrong? (*Crosses back to tray, puts down glasses, etc.*)

OSCAR. There's something wrong with this system, that's what's wrong. I don't think that two single men living alone in a big eight-room apartment should have a cleaner house than my mother.

FELIX. (*Gets rest of dishes, glasses and coasters from table.*) What are you talking about? I'm just going to put the dishes in the sink.

OSCAR. (*Takes his glass which Felix has put on tray and crosses to bar for refill.*) I don't care if you take them to bed with you. You can play Mr. Clean all you want. But don't make *me* feel guilty.

FELIX. (*Takes tray into kitchen, leaving swinging door open.*) I'm not asking you to do it, Oscar. You don't have to clean up.

OSCAR. (*He moves up to the door.*) *That's* why you make me feel guilty. You're always in my bathroom hanging up my towels . . . Whenever I smoke you follow me around with an ashtray . . . Last night I found you washing the kitchen floor shaking your head and moaning, "Footprints, footprints!" (*Paces R.*)

FELIX. (*Comes back to table with silent butler into which he dumps the ashtrays; then wipes them carefully.*) I didn't say they were yours.

OSCAR. (*Angrily; sits D. R. in wing chair.*) Well, they *were* mine, damn it. I have feet and they make prints. What do you want me to do, climb across the cabinets?

FELIX. No! I want you to walk on the floor.

OSCAR. I appreciate that! I really do.

FELIX. (*Crosses to telephone table and clean ashtray there.*) I'm just trying to keep the place livable. I didn't realize I irritated you that much.

OSCAR. I just feel *I* should have the right to decide when my bath-tub needs going over with Dutch Cleanser . . . It's the democratic way!

FELIX. (*Puts down silent butler and rag on coffee table and sits down on couch, glumly.*) I was wondering how long it would take.

OSCAR. How long *what* would take?

FELIX. Before I got on you nerves.

OSCAR. I didn't say you get on my nerves.

FELIX. Well, it's the same thing. You said I irritated you.

OSCAR. *You* said you irritated me. *I* didn't say it.

FELIX. Then what *did* you say?

OSCAR. I don't know *what* I said. What's the difference what I said?

FELIX. It doesn't make any difference. I was just repeating what I thought you said.

OSCAR. Well, don't repeat what you *thought* I said. Repeat what I *said!* . . . My God, that's irritating!

FELX. You see! You *did* say it!

OSCAR. I don't believe this whole conversation. (*Gets up and paces above table.*)

FELIX. (*Pawing with a cup.*) Oscar, I'm—I'm sorry. I don't know what's wrong with me.

OSCAR. (*Paces D. R.*) And don't pout. If you want to fight, we'll fight. But don't pout! Fighting *I* win. Pouting *you* win!

FELIX. You're right. Everything you say about me is absolutely right.

OSCAR. (*Really angry, turn to* Felix.) And don't give in so easily. I'm *not* always right. Sometimes *you're* right.

FELIX. You're right. I do that. I always figure I'm wrong.

OSCAR. Only this time you *are* wrong. And I'm right.

FELIX. Oh, leave me alone.

OSCAR. And don't sulk. That's the same as pouting.

FELIX. I know. I know. (*He squeezes cup with anger.*) Damn me, why can't I do one lousy thing right? (*He suddenly stands up and cocks his arm back angrily about to hurl the cup against the front door, then thinks better of it and puts it down and sits.*)

OSCAR. (*Watching this.*) Why don't you throw it?

FELIX. I almost did. I get so insane with myself sometimes.

OSCAR. Then why don't you throw the cup?

FELIX. Because I'm trying to control myself.

OSCAR. Why?

FELIX. What do you mean, why?

OSCAR. Why do you have to control yourself? You're angry, you felt like throwing the cup, why don't you throw it?

FELIX. Because there's no point to it. I'd still be angry and I'd have a broken cup.

OSCAR. How don't you *know* how you'd feel? Maybe you'd feel *wonderful.* Why do you have to control every single thought in your head? . . . Why don't you let loose once in you life? Do something that you *feel* like doing—and not what you think you're supposed to do. Stop keeping books, Felix. Relax. Get drunk. Get angry . . . C'mon, *break the goddamned cup!*

(Felix suddenly stands up and hurls the cup against the door, smashing it to pieces. Then he grabs his shoulder in pain.)

FELIX. Oww! . . . I hurt my arm! *(Sinks down on couch, massaging his arm.)*

OSCAR. You're hopeless! You're a hopeless mental case! *(Paces about table.)*

From Act II, scene ii:
Oscar and Felix—40-50
Cecily and Gwendolyn—30-35

Cecily and Gwendolyn (the Pigeon sisters) have arrived for dinner. Oscar is buoyantly upbeat at the prospects that lie ahead. Felix, however, is in a snit because—due to Oscar's arriving home late— his London broil is a dry, overcooked lump.

The sisters—young, attractive and very British—enter and small talk is made, Oscar charming them with his cordiality and wit. When he goes to the kitchen to prepare drinks, the ladies are in high sprits, a mood which quickly degenerates due to Felix's sentimental ruminations.

Although the London broil is a burnt offering, this works to an advantage because the obviously promiscuous women invite to boys up to their apartment for dinner.

(The BELL rings.)

FELIX. *(Jumps up.)* Well, they're here. Our dinner guests. I'll get a saw and cut the meat. *(Starts for kitchen.)*

OSCAR. *(Stopping him.)* Stay where you are!

FELIX. I'm not taking the blame for this dinner.

OSCAR. Who's blaming you? Who even cares about the dinner?

FELIX. (*Moves to* Oscar.) I care. I take pride in what I do. And you're going to explain to them exactly what happened.

OSCAR. All right, you can take a Polaroid picture of me coming home at eight o'clock! . . . Now take off that stupid apron because I'm opening the door. (*Rips the towel off* Felix *and goes to the door.*)

FELIX. (*Takes jacket from dining chair and puts it on.*) I just want to get one thing clear. This is the last time I ever cook for you. Because people like you don't even appreciate a decent meal. That's why they have T. V. dinners.

OSCAR. You through?

FELIX. I'm through!

OSCAR. Then smile. (Oscar *smiles and opens the door. The* Girls *poke their heads through the door. They are in their young thirties and somewhat attractive. They are undoubtedly British.*) Well, hello.

GEWNDOLYN. (*To* Oscar.) Hallo!

CECILY. (*To* Oscar.) Hallo.

GWENDOLYN. I do hope we're not late.

OSCAR. No, no. You timed it perfectly. Come on in. (*He points to them as them enter.*) Er, Felix, I'd like you to meet two very good friends of mine, Gwendolyn and Cecily—

CECILY. (*Pointing out his mistake.*) Cecily and Gwendolyn.

OSCAR. Oh, yes. Cecily and Gwendolyn . . . er . . . (*Trying to remember their last name.*) Er . . . Don't tell me . . . Robin? . . . No, no . . . Cardinal?

GWENDOLYN. Wrong both times. It's Pigeon!

OSCAR. Pigeon. Right. Cecily and Gwendolyn Pigeon.

GWENDOLYN. (*To* Felix.) You don't spell it like Walter Pidgeon. You spell it like "Coo Coo" Pigeon.

OSCAR. We'll remember that if it comes up . . . Cecily and Gwendolyn, I'd like you to meet my room-mate . . . and our chef for the evening . . . Felix Unger.

CECILY. (*Holding hand out.*) Heh d'yew dew?

FELIX. (*Moving to her and shaking her hand.*) How do you do?
GWENDOLYN. (*Holding hand out.*) Heh d'yew dew?
FELIX. (*Stepping on landing and shaking her hand.*) How do you do?

(*This puts him nose to nose with* Oscar, *and there is an awkward pause as they look at each other.*)

OSCAR. Well, we did that beautifully . . . Why don't we sit down and make ourselves comfortable?

(Felix *steps aside and ushers the* Girls *down into the room. There is ad-libbing and a bit of confusion and milling around as they* All *squeeze between the arm-chair and the couch. And the* Pigeons *finally seat themselves on the couch.* Oscar *sits in the armchair and* Felix *sneaks past him to the love seat. Finally* All *have settled down.*)

CECILY. This is ever so nice, isn't it, Gwen?
GEWNDOLYN. (*Looking around.*) Lovely. And much nicer than our flat. Do you have help?
OSCAR. Er, yes, I have a man who comes in every night.
CECILY. Aren't you the lucky one?

(Cecily, Gwendolyn *and* Oscar *all laugh at her joke.* Oscar *looks over at* Felix *but there is no response.*)

OSCAR. (*Rubs hands together.*) Well, isn't this nice? . . . I was telling Felix yesterday how we happened to meet.
GWENDOLYN. Oh? . . . Who's Felix?
OSCAR. (*A little embarrassed. Points to* Felix.) He is!
GWENDOLYN. Oh, yes, of course. I'm so sorry.

(Felix *nods that it's all right.*)

CECILY. You know it happened to us again this morning.

OSCAR. What did?

GWENDOLYN. Stuck in the elevator again.

OSCAR. Really? Just the two of you?

CECILY. And poor old Mr. Kessler from the third floor. We were in there half an hour.

OSCAR. No kidding? What happened?

GEWNDOLYN. Not much, I'm afraid..

(Cecily *and* Gwendolyn *both laugh at her latest joke, joined by* Oscar. *He once again looks over at* Felix, *but there is no response.*)

OSCAR. (*Rubs hands again.*) Well, this is really nice.

CECILY. And ever so much cooler than our place.

GWENDOLYN. It's like equatorial Africa on our side of the building.

CECILY. Last night it was so bad Gwen and I sat there in Nature's Own cooling ourselves in front of the open frig. Can you imagine such a thing?

OSCAR. Er . . . I'm working on it.

GWENDOLYN. Actually, it's impossible to get a night's sleep. Cec and I really don't know what to do.

OSCAR. Why don't you sleep with an air conditioner?

GWENDOLYN. We haven't got one.

OSCAR. But we have.

GWENDOLYN. Oh you! I told you about that one, didn't I, Cec?

FELIX. They say it may rain Friday.

(*They* All *stare at* Felix.)

GWENDOLYN. Oh?

CECILY. That should cool things off a bit.

OSCAR. I wouldn't be surprised.

FELIX. Although sometimes it gets hotter after it rains.

GWENDOLYN. Yes, it does, doesn't it?

(*The continue to stare at* Felix.)

FELIX. (*Jumps up and, picking up ladle, starts for the kitchen.*) Dinner is served!

OSCAR. (*Stopping him.,*) No, it's isn't! I'm sure the girls would like a cocktail first. (*To* Girls.) Wouldn't you, girls?

GWENDOLYN. Well, we wouldn't put up a struggle.

OSCAR. There you are. (*To* Cecily.) What would you like?

CECILY. Oh, I really don't know. (*To* Oscar.) What have you got?

FELIX. London broil.

OSCAR. (*To* Felix.) She means to drink. (*To* Cecily.) We have everything. And what we don't have, I'll mix in the medicine cabinet. What'll it be? (*Crouches next to her.*)

CECILY. Oh . . . a double vodka.

GEWNDOLYN. Cecily . . . not before dinner.

CECILY. (*To the* Men.) My sister . . . She watches over me like a mother hen. (*To* Oscar.) Make it a *small* double vodka.

OSCAR. A small double vodka! . . . And for the beautiful mother hen?

GWENDOLYN. Oh . . . I'd like something cool. I think I would like to have a double Drambuie with some crushed ice . . . unless you don't have the crushed ice.

OSCAR. I was up all night with a sledge hammer. . . I shall return! (*Goes to the bar and gets bottles of vodka and Drambuie.*)

FELIX. (*Going to him.*) Where are you going?

OSCAR. To get the refreshments.

FELIX. (*Starting to panic.*) Inside? What'll *I* do?

OSCAR. You can finish your weather report. (*He exits into kitchen.*)

FELIX. (*Calls after him.*) Don't forget to look at my meat! (*He turns and faces the* Girls. *He crosses to chair and sits. He crosses legs nonchalantly. But he is ill at ease and he crosses them again. He is becoming aware of the silence and he can no longer get away with just smiling.*) Er . . . Oscar tells me you're sisters.

CECILY. Yes. That's right. (*She looks at* Gwendolyn.)

FELIX. From England.

GWENDOLYN. Yes. That's right. (*She looks at* Cecily.)

FELIX. I see. (*Silence. Then, his little joke.*) We're not brothers.

CECILY. Yes. We know.

FELIX. Although I am a brother. I have a brother who's a doctor. He lives in Buffalo. That's upstate New York.

GWENDOLYN. (*Taking cigarette from her purse.*) Yes, we know.

FELIX. You know my brother?

GWENDOLYN. No. We know Buffalo is upstate in New York.

FELIX. Oh! (*Gets up, takes a cigarette lighter from side table and lights* Gwendolyn's *cigarette.*)

CECILY. We've been there! . . . Have you?

FELIX. No! . . . Is it nice?

CECILY. Lovely.

(Felix *closes lighter on cigarette and turns to go back to chair, taking the cigarette, now caught in the lighter, with him. He notices the cigarette and hastily gives it back to* Gwendolyn, *stopping to light it once again. He puts lighter back on table and sits nervously. There is a pause.*)

FELIX. Isn't this interesting? . . . How long have you been in the United States of America?

CECILY. Almost four years now.

FELIX. (*Nods.*) Uh-huh. . . Just visiting?

GWENDOLYN. (*Looks at* Cecily.) No! . . . We live here.

FELIX. And you work here too, do you?

CECILY. Yes. We're secretaries for Slenderama.

GWENDOLYN. You know. The health club.

CECILY. People bring us their bodies and we do wonderful things with them.

GWENDOLYN. Actually, if you're interested, we can get you ten percent off.

CECILY. Off the price, not your body.

FELIX. Yes, I see. (*He laughs, they* All *laugh. Suddenly shouts towards kitchen.*) Oscar, where's the drinks?

OSCAR. (*Offstage.*) Coming! Coming!

CECILY. What field of endeavor are you engaged in?

FELIX. I write news for CBS.

CECILY. Oh! Fascinating!

GWENDOLYN. Where do you get your ideas from?

FELIX. (*He looks at her as though she's a Martian.*) From the news.

GWENDOLYN. Oh, yes, of course. Silly Me. . .

CECILY. Maybe you can mention Gwen and me in one of your news reports.

FELIX. Well, if you do something spectacular, maybe I will.

CECILY. Oh, we're done spectacular things, but I don't think we' d want it spread all over the Telly, do you, Gwen?

(*They both laugh.*)

FELIX. (*He laughs too, then cries out almost for help.*) Oscar!

OSCAR. (*Offstage.*) Yeah yeah!

FELIX. (*To* Girls.) It's such a large apartment, sometimes you have to shout.

GWEWDOLYN. Just you two baches live here?

FELIX. Baches? Oh, bachelors! We're not bachelors. We're divorced. That is, Oscar's divorced. I'm *getting* a divorced.

CECILY. Oh. Small world. We're cut the dinghy loose too, as they say.

GWENDOLYN. Well, you couldn't have a *better* matched foursome, could you?

FELIX. (*Smiles weakly.*) No, I suppose not.

GWENDOLYN. Although technically, I'm a widow. I was divorcing my husband but he died before the final papers came through.

FELIX. Oh, I'm awfully sorry. (*Sighs.*) It's a terrible thing, isn't it? Divorce.

GWENDOLYN. It can be . . . if you haven't got the right solicitor.

CECILY. That's true. Sometimes they can drag it out for months. I was lucky. Snip, cut and I was free.

FELIX. I mean it's terrible what it can do to people. After all, what is divorce? It's taking two happy people and tearing their lives completely apart. It's inhuman, don't you think so?

CECILY. Yes, it can be an awful bother.

GWENDOLYN. But of course, that's all water under the bridge now eh? . . . er . . . I'm terribly sorry, but I think I've forgotten your name.

FELIX. Felix.

GWENDOLYN. Oh, yes. Felix.

CECILY. Like the cat.

(Felix *takes wallet from his jacket pocket.*)

GWENDOLYN. Well, the Pigeons will have to beware of the cat, won't they? (*She laughs.*)

CECILY. (*Nibbles on a nut from the dish.*) Mmm, cashews. Lovely.

FELIX. (*Takes snapshot out of wallet.*) This is the worst part of breaking up. (*He hands picture to* Cecily.)

CECILY. (*Looks at it.*) Childhood sweethearts, were you?

FELIX. No, no. That's my little boy and girl. (Cecily *gives the picture to* Gwendolyn, *and takes a pair of glasses from her purse and puts them on.*) He's seven, she's five.

CECILY. (*Looks again.*) Oh! Sweet.

FELIX. They live with their mother.

GWENDOLYN. I imagine you must miss them terribly.

FELIX. (*Takes back the picture and looks at it longingly.*) I can't stand being away from them. (*Shrugs.*) But—that's what happens with divorce.

CECILY. When do you get to see them?

FELIX. Every night. I stop on my way home! . . . Then I take them on weekends and I get them on holidays and July and August.

CECILY. Oh! . . . Well, when is it that you miss them?

FELIX. Whenever I'm not there. If they didn't have to go to school so early, I'd go over and make them breakfast. They love my French toast.

GWENDOLYN. You're certainly a devoted father.

FELIX. It's Frances who's the wonderful one.

CECILY. She's the little girl?

FELIX. No. She's the mother. My wife.

GWENDOLYN. The one you're divorcing?

FELIX. (*Nods.*) Mm! . . . She's done a terrific job bringing them up. They always looks so nice. They're so polite. Spell beautifully. Never "yeah." Always "yes." . . . They're such good kids. And she did it all. She's the kind of woman who—Ah, what am I saying? You don't want to hear any of this. (*Puts picture back in wallet.*)

CECILY. Nonsense. You have a right to be proud. You have two beautiful children and a wonderful ex-wife.

FELIX. (*Containing his emotions.*) I know. I know. (*He hands* Cecily *another snapshot.*) That's her. Frances.

GWENDOLYN. (*Looking at picture.*) Oh, she's pretty. Isn't she pretty, Cecy?

CECILY. Oh, yes. Pretty. A pretty girl. Very pretty.

FELIX. (*Takes picture back.*) Thank you. (*Shows them another snapshot.*) Isn't this nice?

GWENDOLYN. (*Looks.*) There's no one in the picture.

FELIX. I know. It's a picture of our living room. We had a beautiful apartment.

GWENDOLYN. Oh, yes, Pretty. Very pretty.

CECILY. Those are lovely lamps.

FELIX. Thank you! (*Takes picture.*) We bought them in Mexico on our honeymoon . . . (*He looks at picture again.*) I used to love to come home at night. (*He's beginning to break.*) That was my whole life. My wife, my kids . . . and my apartment. (*He breaks down and sobs.*)

CECILY. Does she have the lamps now, too?

FELIX. (*Nods.*) I gave her everything . . . It'll never be like that again . . . Never! . . . I—I— (*He turns head away.*) I'm sorry. (*He takes out a handkerchief and dabs eyes.*) Please forgive me. I didn't mean to get emotional. (*Trying to pull himself together. He picks up bowl from side table and offers it to* Girls.) Would you like some potato chips?

(Cecily *takes the bowl.*)

GWENDOLYN. You mustn't be ashamed. I think it's a rare quality in a man to be able to cry.

FELIX. (*Hand over eyes.*) Please. Let's not talk about it.

CECILY. I think it's sweet. Terribly sweet. (*Takes potato chip.*)

FELIX. You're just making it worse.

GWENDOLYN. (*Teary-eyed.*) It's so refreshing to hear a man speak so highly of the woman he's divorcing! . . . Oh, dear. (*She takes out her handkerchief.*) Now you're got me thinking about poor Sydney.

CECILY. Oh, Gwen. Please don't. (*Puts bowl down.*)

GWENDOLYN. It was a good marriage at first. Everyone said so. Didn't they, Cecily? Not like you and George.

CECILY. (*The past returns as she comforts* Gwendolyn.) That's right. George and I were never happy . . . Not for one single, solitary day. (*She remembers her unhappiness and grabs her handkerchief and dabs here eyes.* All Three *are now sitting with handkerchiefs at their eyes.*)

FELIX. Isn't this ridiculous?

GWENDOLYN. I don't know what brought this on. I was feeling so good a few minutes ago.

CECILY. I haven't cried since I was fourteen.

GWENDOLYN. Oh dear oh dear oh dear.

(All Three *sit sobbing into their handkerchiefs. Suddenly* Oscar *bursts happily into the room with a tray full of drinks. He is all smiles.*)

OSCAR. (*Like a corny M.C.*) Is ev-rybuddy happy? (*Then he sees the maudlin scene.* Felix *and the* Girls *quickly try to pull themselves together.*) What the hell happened?

FELIX. Nothing! Nothing! (*He quickly puts handkerchief away.*)

OSCAR. What do you mean, nothing? I'm gone three minutes and I walk into a funeral parlor. What did you say to them?

FELIX. I didn't say anything. Don't start in again, Oscar.

OSCAR. I can't leave you alone for five seconds. Well, if you really want to cry, go inside and look at your London broil.

FELIX. (*He rushes madly into the kitchen.*) Oh, my gosh! Why didn't you call me? I told you to call me.

OSCAR. (*Giving drink to* Cecily.) I'm sorry, girls. I forgot to warn you about Felix. He's a walking soap opera.

GWENDOLYN. I think he's the dearest thing I ever met.

CECILY. (*Taking the glass.*) He's so sensitive. So fragile. I just want to bundle him up in my arms and take care of him.

OSCAR. (*Holds out* Gwendolyn's *drink. At this, he puts it back down on tray and takes a swallow from his own drink.*) Well, I think when he comes out of that kitchen you may have to.

(*Sure enough,* Felix *comes out of the kitchen onto the landing looking like a wounded puppy. With a protective kitchen glove, he holds a pan with the exposed London broil.* Black *is the color of his true love.*)

FELIX. (*Very Calmly.*) I'm going down to the delicatessen. I'll be right back.

OSCAR. (*Going to him.*) Wait a minute. Maybe it's not so bad. Let's see it.

FELIX. (*Shows him.*) Here! Look! Nine dollars and thirty-four cents' worth of ashes! (*Pulls pan away. To* Girls.) I'll get some corned beef sandwiches.

OSCAR. (*Trying to get a look at it.*) Give it to me! Maybe we can save some of it.

FELIX. (*Holding it away from* Oscar.) There's nothing to save. It's all black meat. Nobody likes black meat! . . .

OSCAR. Can't I even look at it?

FELIX. No, you can't look at it!

OSCAR. Why can't I look at it?

FELIX. If you looked at your watch before you wouldn't have to look at the black meat now! Leave it alone! (*Turns to go back into kitchen.*)

GWENDOLYN. (*Going to him.*) Felix . . . ! Can *we* look at it?

CECILY. (*Turning to him, kneeling on couch.*) Please? (Felix *stops in the doorway to kitchen. He hesitates for a moment. He likes them. Then he turns and wordlessly holds pan to them.* Gwendolyn *and* Cecily *inspect it wordlessly, and then turn away sobbing quietly. To* Oscar.) How about Chinese food?

OSCAR. A wonderful idea.

GWENDOLYN. I've got a better idea. Why don't we just make pot luck in the kitchen?

OSCAR. A *much* better idea.

FELIX. I used up all the pots! (*Crosses to love seat and sits, still holding the pan.*)

CECILY. Well then, we can eat up in our place. We have tons of Horn and Hardart's.

OSCAR. (*Gleefully.*) That's the best idea I ever heard.

GWENDOLYN. Of course it's awfully hot up there. You'll have to take off your jackets.

OSCAR. (*Smiling.*) We can always open up the refrigerator.

CECILY. (*Gets purse from couch.*) Give us five minutes to get into our cooking things.

(*Gwendolyn gets purse from couch.*)

OSCAR. Can't you make it four? I'm suddenly starving to death.

(*The* Girls *are crossing to door.*)

GWENDOLYN. Don't forget the wine.

OSCAR. How could I forget the wine?

CECILY. And a corkscrew.

OSCAR. *And* a corkscrew.

GWENDOLYN. And Felix.

OSCAR. No, I won't forget Felix.

CECILY. Ta ta!
OSCAR. Ta ta!
GWENDOLYN. Ta ta!

(*The* Girls *exit.*)

THE STAR-SPANGLED GIRL

Premièred December 21, 1966
at the Plymouth Theatre, New York City

Directed by George Axelrod

CAST

Andy Hobart	Anthony Perkins
Norman Cornell	Richard Benjamin
Sophie Rauschmeyer	Connie Stevens

The action of the play takes place in a studio apartment in San Francisco.

Andy Hobart and Norman Cornell are financially strapped, idealistic young men who are, in spite of overwhelming odds, committed to publishing the protest magazine *Fallout*. That is, until Sophie Rauschmeyer, a sexy, athletic, all-American girl moves into their building and Norman falls obsessively in love with her—even her smell sends him into rapture. His runaway passion angers Sophie and interferes with his writing for *Fallout*. Whereas Norman is deliriously enamored of Sophie, Andy finds her a narrow-minded throwback and a distraction that threatens the life of their publication.

After Sophie loses her job thanks to Norman's outlandish behavior, Andy hires her as a means of securing Norman's productivity. But this plan is doomed because Norman cannot keep his hands off of the girl. And when Sophie reads *Fallout,* she and Andy engage in verbal crossfire generated by a diverse set of political attitudes. She sees Andy as a traitor and Communist. He views her as a provincial, narrow-minded rustic. Then, in an unexpected twist, Sophie confesses, in spite of their political dichotomy, that she finds Andy physically irresistible. Norman returns to find them kissing.

Norman, angered at finding Sophie in Andy's arms, is leaving. The threat of his departure generates a spirited argument between them, and Andy, bent upon getting out the next issue of *Fallout,* handcuffs Norman to a steam pipe. Enter Sophie. She is returning to Hunnicut, Arkansas, to train for the Olympics because she realizes that her feelings for Andy will go unrequited. Upon her departure, Andy releases Norman, announces that he is going to scrub the publication and return to Philadelphia, and confesses that he needs Sophie. Sophie, listening at the door, returns and differences are reconciled. At play's end, Sophie is back on the job dusting the apartment, Andy is concentrating on a clipboard, and Norman is flailing away at the typewriter. Sophie and Andy are an item, Norman has returned to earth, and *Fallout* will be getting out on time.

From Act II, scene i:
Sophie—20-25
Andy—20-30

Norman's obsessive love-sick forays at the YMCA have caused Sophie to lose her job there. In this scene, Sophie, soaking wet from hastily leaving the Y's swimming pool, has returned to Andy's and Norman's apartment furious, ready to do battle. Andy, as a means of mollifying her anger, hires her to work on their activist rag Fallout.

(Norman *disappears through door at the top of ladder. The doorbell buzzes again.* Andy *goes to the door and opens it.* Sophie *enters—wet. Carries a YMCA duffel bag and a copy of* Fallout.)

SOPHIE. (*Goes to foot of stairs.*) Where is he? Where is that insane, crazy, tresspassin' lunatic? (Andy *closes the door.*) I know exactly what I'm going to do to him. I planned it all as I sat there drippin' all over the bus.

ANDY. (*Goes toward her.*) He's up on the roof, miserable and eating his heart out.

SOPHIE. Well, you can tell him not to bother. Ah'm gonna get a bird dog to eat it out for him . . . Ah have been fired. They didn't even give me time to dry off.

ANDY. I know. I just spoke to the "Y." But it wasn't your fault. Didn't you explain that to them?

SOPHIE. Ah found it difficult getting their attention while a crazy man was chasing me all through the YWCA . . . And that present of his is still pecking away at everyone in the building.

ANDY. What present?

SOPHIE. The duck. He bought me a live duck. It's still there quackin' and snappin' at everyone. When ah left, the gym teacher was a-hanging from the basketball hoop and then that crazy bird chased a seventy-three year old Arts and Crafts teacher down to the swimmin' pool and off the high diving board.

ANDY. I didn't know about that.

SOPHIE. Well, did you know that ah've been locked out of mah apartment until ah pay mah rent which ah can't do because ah don't have a job.

ANDY. Look, we'll make it up to you somehow. I'll get you another job. Just give me a couple of days.

SOPHIE. (*Goes L., D. of* Andy.) Ah don't have a couple of days. Ah have rent to pay and food to buy. What am ah gonna do?

ANDY. There must be someone in San Francisco who needs somebody young and healthy and strong . . . I don't suppose you've ever considered professional football?

SOPHIE. (*Goes D. to phone on desk and starts to dial.*) Ah'm callin' my fiance!

ANDY. (*Goes toward* Sophie.) Wait . . . I have an idea. I don't say you're going to love it, but how would you like to come to work for us?

SOPHIE. Ah would rather get beaten in the Olympics by Red China.

ANDY. Why not? It'll pay your rent and buy you your iron and steel, or whatever it is you eat.

SOPHIE. (*Hangs up.*) Ah believe you're serious. If you're serious, I suggest you make yourself available for our country's mental health program. Do you think I would work for that bomb aimed at the heart of America?

ANDY. What bomb?

SOPHIE. (*Takes a few steps R. to* Andy.) Mr. Hobart, ah don't know if you're a communist, or a fascist, or just a plain old-fashioned traitor . . . But you are certainly no American.

ANDY. I don't know what you're talking about, but writing constructive criticism about the degenerating American way of life is certainly not treason.

SOPHIE. I don't know what is in your government overthrowing mind, but do you expect me to work for a magazine that publishes an article entitled . . . (*Goes R., U of* Andy, *looks through pages.*) . . . "Is L.B.J. on L.S.D?"

ANDY. We're not implying that he takes drugs. It's a symbolic alliteration meaning maybe the President in certain areas has gone too far.

SOPHIE. How about . . . "Twenty-Seven Ways to Burn a Wet Draft Card?" . . . Written from personal experience, Mr. Hobart?

ANDY. For your information, I happened to have served two years in the United States Army where I was interpreter for Brigadier General Walker Cooper.

SOPHIE. In what country?

ANDY. In *this* country. That idiot could hardly speak English! (*Tosses magazine on table.*) . . . My feelings about this country run just a deeply as yours, but if you'll turn down the national anthem for a few minutes, you'll be able to hear what some of the people are complaining about.

SOPHIE. Well, ah am one of the people and *yew* are one of the things ah'm complaining about.

ANDY. Well, fortunately, you're not in much of a position to complain about *anything!* . . . Look, if you don't work, you don't eat. If you don't eat, you get very skinny, you fall down and then you're dead. (*Goes L., U. of pole table.*) If you think your Marine will be happy living with a dead, skinny lady, that's his business. Personally, I think you ought to accept the meager bread I'm offering you.

SOPHIE. First you take away my loaf and then you offer me your meager bread.

ANDY. Why does everything you say sound like it came out of the Bible?

SOPHIE. Thank goodness yew heard of the book.

ANDY. Look, do you want the job or don't you? If you don't want it, *I'll* take it 'cause I need the money.

SOPHIE. Unfortunately, so do I. Just tell me why . . . why do yew want me around here?

ANDY. I'll tell you why. I *don't* want you around here. But that nut up on the hot tin roof wants you around here. You believe in your principles, I believe in mine. Mine is this magazine and I'll do anything from keeping it from going under water . . . That was an unfortunate choice of phrase.

SOPHIE. All right. That's your principle. Mah principle is breathing, eating and living, just like any other animal on this earth.

ANDY. So much for your character references. Now about salary. What did you get at the "Y?"

SOPHIE. Seventy-two dollars.

ANDY. Norman and I both know how to swim. I'll give you fifty-five.

SOPHIE. For fifty-five dollars ah will come in early and poison your coffee. Ah want what ah got at the "Y." Seventy-two dollars.

Andy. (*Reluctantly.*) So be it, you're hired. Your hours will be from ten to six, half a day on Saturday. Can you type?

SOPHIE. No.

ANDY. Can't you take shorthand?

SOPHIE. No.

ANDY. Can you do filing?

SOPHIE. No.

ANDY. Maybe you'd better come in at eleven . . . Can you cook?

SOPHIE. Mah cat seems to think so.

ANDY. Okay, you can make lunches and pretend to look busy. Let's say you have two main functions. First, to keep out of my way at all times, and second, to *smile* at Norman as much as is humanly possible.

SOPHIE. Yes, sir. The first ah will do with the utmost dedication. And the second ah will do over mah dead body.

ANDY. (*Goes R., D of* Sophie.) Miss Rauschmeyer, it's evident you and I haven't gotten along since you came to work here . . . We're both trying to make the best out of an impossible situation. You need money, I need you to say Goo-Goo to my partner once in a while. Now I suggest you roll up your lips and smile so we can get to work.

SOPHIE. All right, ah'll make mah bargain with the devil. Ah've never run from a fight. Ah'm ready to go to work. (*She extends her hand.*)

ANDY. Am I supposed to shake that?

SOPHIE. No, you're supposed to put seventy-two dollars in it.

ANDY. We pay at the end of the week. Company policy.

SOPHIE. Then ah'll start at the end of the week. Ah-don't-trust your policy.

ANDY. All right, wait a minute. (*He crosses to side and gets milk bottles filled with pennies.*) There's seventy dollars in pennies. (*He gives her two bottles, takes third bottle and empties some of it in can on sofa.*) Minus Federal withholding tax and social security.

PLAZA SUITE

(L)

Premièred February 14, 1968
at the Plymouth Theatre, New York City

Directed by Mike Nichols

CAST

"Visitor from Mamaroneck"

Bellhop	Bob Balaban
Karen Nash	Maureen Stapleton
Sam Nash	George C. Scott
Waiter	Jose Ocasio
Jean McCormack	Claudette Nevins

"Visitor from Hollywood"

Waiter	Jose Ocasio
Jesse Kiplinger	George C. Scott
Muriel Tate	Maureen Stapleton

"Visitor from Forest Hills"

Norma Hubley	Maureen Stapleton
Roy Hubley	George C. Scott
Bordern Isler	Bob Balaban
Mimsey Hubley	Claudett Nevins

Plaza Suite is comprised of three one-act plays whose action takes place in Suite 719 at the Plaza Hotel, New York City.

"The Visitor from Mamaroneck."

While Karen and Sam Nash are having their house painted, they take a suite at the Plaza until the work is completed. Karen, sensing an opportunity to revitalize romantic juices, books Suite 719, the room she and Sam had occupied on their wedding night. But Sam is not romantically inclined. Sadly, Karen's desire for intimacy is dashed, and the evening becomes one of verbal fencing and petty bickering during which the fragile state of their marriage surfaces.

Sam's secretary, Jean, arrives with important papers to sign. She is young, attractive and slim. They confer, and business matters necessitate that Sam return to his office that evening. When Karen asks Sam if he is having an affair with Jean, he vehemently denies it, but, upon further probing, admits to the relationship. Karen feigns understanding, but underneath she is hurting and wishes to salvage their marriage of twenty-three years. She begs Sam not to go to his office, where he will be working late with Jean, but Sam, after vacillating, tells her that he has to go.

From Act I:
Karen and Sam—45-55

The fact of Sam's affair with his secretary has been disclosed. Although Karen plays the forgiving wife, she is deeply hurt and untimely pleads with Sam to stay. But he departs, leaving the action beyond the play in an ambiguous state.

SAM. (*Gets up, takes case and crosses to door.*) You're driving me right out of here, you know that, don't you?

KAREN. There'll always be room for you in my garage.

SAM. I walk out this door now, I don't come back.

KAREN. I think you will.

SAM. What makes you so sure?

KAREN. You forgot to take your eye drops.

SAM. (*He storms to coffee table, snatches up drops and crosses back to door.*) Before I go I just want to say one thing. Whatever you think of me is probably true. No, not probably, *definitely.* I have been a bastard right from the beginning. I don't expect you to forgive me.

KAREN. But I do.

SAM. (*Whirling back to her.*) Let me finish. I don't expect you to forgive me. But I ask you with all conscience, with all your understanding, not to blame Jean for any of this.

KAREN. (*Collapses on couch. Then pulling herself together.*) I'll send her a nice gift.

SAM. (*Puts down case beside sofa.*) She's been torturing herself ever since this started. *I'm* the one who forced the issue.

KAREN. (*Moving away from him on sofa, mimics* Jean.) "It didn't show up on the 1400 but I rechecked it with my own files and made the correction on the 640." . . . You know as well as I do that's code for "I'll meet you at the Piccadilly Hotel."

SAM. (*Kneeling beside sofa.*) You won't believe me, will you? That she's a nice girl?

KAREN. Nice for you and nice for me are two different things.

SAM. If it's that Sunday supplement psychology you're using, Karen, it's backfiring because you're just making it easier for me.

KAREN. Well, you like things easy, don't you? You don't even have an affair the hard way.

SAM. Meaning what?

KAREN. (*Getting up.*) Meaning that you could have at least taken the trouble to look outside your office for a girl . . . (*Picks up imagi-*

nary phone.) "Miss McCormack, would you please come inside and take an affair!" . . . Honestly, Sam. (*Moves above sofa.*)

SAM. Karen, don't force me to say nice things about her to you.

KAREN. I can't help it. I'm just disappointed in you. It's so damned unoriginal.

SAM. What did you want her to be, a fighter pilot with the Israeli Air Force?

KAREN. *Everyone* cheats with their secretary. I expected more from *my* husband.

SAM. (*Shaking his head.*) I never saw you like this. You live with a person your whole life, you don't really know them.

KAREN. (*Crossing below sofa to bedroom.*) Go on, Sam, go have your little affair. You are fifty-one years old. In an hour it may be too late. (*Sits at dresser, and brushes hair.*)

SAM. (*Getting up and crossing to her in bedroom.*) By God, you are something. You are really something special, Karen. Twenty-three years I'm married to you and I still can't make you out. You don't look much different than the ordinary woman but I promise you there is nothing walking around on two legs that compares in any way, shape or form to the likes of you.

KAREN. (*Drops brush and turns to him. Laughing.*) So if I'm so special, what are you carrying on with secretaries for?

SAN. I'll be God-damned if I know . . .

(*They look at each other. He turns and starts to front door, taking attaché case.*)

KAREN. (*Following him into the living room.*) Sam! (Sam *stops.*) Sam . . . do I still have my two choices? (*He turns and looks at her.*) Because if I do . . . I chose "Get rid of Miss McCormack. (*He looks away.*) I pick "Stay here and work it out with me, Sam." (Karen *turns her back to him and leans against the arm of the sofa.*) Because

the other way I think I'm going to lose. Don't go to the office tonight, Sam . . . Stay with me . . . Please.

SAM. (*He moves about indecisively.*) Maybe tomorrow, Karen . . . I
can't—tonight! (*He opens door.*) I'll—I'll see you.

KAREN. When? (*He exits, leaving door open.*) Never mind. I love
surprises.

"Visitor from Hollywood."

*While in New York on business, big-time movie producer Jesse
Kiplinger phones his high-school sweetheart, Muriel Tate. He is a
jaded denizen of the Hollywood scene and disillusioned with the
women in his life. In Muriel he looks forward to an afternoon of
harmless sex with a woman still demure and unaffected. But reality
proves otherwise. Muriel, a heavy drinker, locked in an unhappy
marriage, is far from the sweet innocent he knew at Tenafly High.*

From Act II:
Muriel and Jessie—35-45

*Muriel, feeling the effects of alcohol, is far from the happy housewife
she claims.*

(*Muriel drinks. Jessie crosses to her, touches her.*)

JESSIE. How are you, Muriel?

MURIEL. Happy? . . . Oh, yes. I think if I'm anything, I'm happy.
(*Moves D. to sofa.*)

JESSIE. I'm glad. You deserve happiness, Muriel.

MURIEL. Yes, Larry and I are very happy . . . (*She Drinks.*) I would
have to say that Larry and I have one of the happier marriages in
Tenafly. (*She drinks again.*)

JESSIE. That's wonderful.

MURIEL. I mean we've had our ups and downs like any married couple but I think in the final analysis what's left is . . . that we're happy.

JESSIE. (*Moves D. to bar.*) I couldn't be more pleased. Well, listen, it's no surprise. Larry's a wonderful guy.

MURIEL. Do you think so?

JESSIE. Don't you?

MURIEL. Yes, *I* do. But no one else seems to care for him. (*Sits on sofa.*) Of course they don't know him the way *I* do. I'm out of stinger gain. (*Holds glass out to* Jessie.)

JESSIE. (*Takes her glass.*) Are you sure you're going to be all right? I mean driving?

MURIEL. (*Gradually feeling the effects of the drinks.*) If I had to worry about getting home every time I had three Vodka stingers, I'd give up driving. (Jessie *crosses to bar, looking back at her in puzzlement.*) Yes, I'd say that in spite of everything, Larry and I have worked out happiness . . . or some form of it.

JESSIE.   Is he doing well in business? (*Fills glass once again.*)

MURIEL. Oh, in business you don't have to worry. In that department he's doing great. I mean he's really got a wonderful business there . . . Of course, it was good when my father had it. (Jessie *hands her drink.*) Ooh, cheers. (*She drinks.*)

JESSIE. (*Sitting on arm of sofa.*) In what department isn't he doing well?

MURIEL. He's doing well in *every* department.

JESSIE. Are you sure?

MURIEL. I'm positive.

JESSIE. Then I'm glad.

MURIEL. Why, what did you hear?

JESSIE. I haven't heard a thing except what you're telling me.

MURIEL. Well, I'm telling you that we have a happy marriage. Are you trying to infer that we don't have a happy marriage?

JESSIE. No . . .

MURIEL. Well, you're wrong. We have a happy marriage. A Goddamned happy marriage. (*Tries to put glass down on table, misses and nearly slips off sofa.*) Oh, I'm sorry. I should have had lunch.

JESSIE. (*Steadies her and picks up glass from floor and puts it on table.*) Shall I order down for some food?

MURIEL. No, I can't stay. Larry'll be home about five.

JESSIE. I thought he comes home at seven.

MURIEL. If he comes home at all . . . Please forgive me, Jessie, I seem to be losing control of myself.

JESSIE. You drank those too quickly. Didn't you have anything to eat all day?

MURIEL. Just an olive with the two stingers I had downstairs . . . I'll be all right.

JESSIE. Do you want to lie down for a while?

MURIEL. What's the point? You're going back to Hollywood in a few days . . . Oh, I see what you mean . . . Oh, God, I'm sorry, Jessie, I seem to be running off at the mouth.

JESSIE. (*Sits down next to her.*) What is it, Muriel? What's with you and Larry?

MURIEL. Nothing. I told you, we're very happy. We have tiny, little differences like every normal couple but basically we're very happy together. I couldn't ask for a better life . . . (*And she throws her arms around* Jessie *and gives him a full, passionate kiss on the lips, then she pulls away.*) Oh, you shouldn't have done that, Jessie. I'm very vulnerable right now and you mustn't take advantage . . . I'm going. I've got to go. (*Gets up and moves away.*)

"Visitor from Forest Hills."

On her wedding day, Mimsey Hubley has locked herself in the bathroom. Downstairs in the Green Room awaits groom Borden Eisler and his family along with sixty-eight guests, nine waiters, a photographer, and four musicians—not to mention a fortune in spoiling hors d'oeuvres. Mother and father stall, but Mimsey is intractable. She remains locked in the bathroom as Norma and Roy Hubley grow more frustrated and panicked with each passing second. After a seemingly interminable period during which Roy nearly breaks his arm, falls from a seven-story ledge, rips his rented tux, and Norma rips her hose and nearly succumbs to anxiety, Mimsey emerges from the john at her fiancé's terse command, "Cool it." Mimsey's reluctance to leave the bathroom stemmed from a fear for what she and Borden might become—a disgruntled, bickering couple. Like her parents.

From Act III:
Norma—40-50
Roy—45-50

Norma and Roy have exhausted every verbal argument in attempting to convince Mimsey to leave the bathroom and Roy, frustrated and angry, is through with cajoling—he's going to break down the door. But Roy injures his arm in the attempt, a turn of events unleashing even greater frustration, bickering and blaming.

(Norma *gets out of the way as* Roy *hurls his body, led by his shoulder with fill force against the door. It doesn't budge. He stays against the door silently a second, he doesn't react. Then he says calmly and softly:*)

ROY. Get a doctor.

NORMA. (*Standing below door.*) I knew it. I knew it.

ROY. (*Drawing back from door.*) Don't tell me I knew it, just get a doctor. (*Through door.*) I'm not coming in, Mimsey, because my arm is broken.

NORMA. Let me see it. Can you move your fingers? (*Moves to him and examines his fingers.*)

ROY. (*Through door.*) Are you happy now? Your mother has torn stocking and your father has a broken arm. How much longer is this gonna go on?

NORMA. (*Moving* Roy's *fingers.*) It's not broken, you can move your fingers. Give me four dollars with your other hand, I have to get stockings. (*Starts to go into his pockets. He slaps her hand away.*)

ROY. Are you crazy moving a broken arm?

NORMA. Two dollars. I'll get a cheap pair.

ROY. (*As though she were a lunatic.*) I'm not carrying any cash to-day. Rented, everything is rented.

NORMA. I can't rent stockings. Don't you even have a charge-plate? (*Starts to go through his pockets again.*)

ROY. (*Slaps her hand away. Then pointing dramatically.*) Wait in the Green Room! You're no use to me here, go wait in the Green Room!

NORMA. With torn stockings?

ROY. Stand behind the rented potted plant. (*Takes her by the arm and leads her below bed. Confidentially.*) They're going to call from downstairs any second asking where the bride is. And *I'm* the one who's going to have to speak to them. Me! Me! ME! (*The* Phone rings. *Pushing her toward phone.*) That's them. *You* speak to them!

NORMA. What happened to *me me me?*

(*The* Phone *rings again.*)

ROY. (*Moving to bathroom door.*) Answer it. Answer it. (*The* Phone *rings again.*)

NORMA. (*Moving to phone.*) What am I going to say to them?

ROY. I don't know. Maybe something will come to you as you're talking.

NORMA. (*Picks up phone.*) Hello? . . . Oh, Mr. Eisler . . . Yes, it certainly is the big moment. (*She forces a merry laugh.*)

ROY. Stall 'em. Stall 'em. Just keep stalling him. What ever you do, stall 'em! (*Turns to door.*)

NORMA. (*On phone.*) Yes, we'll be down in two minutes. (*Hangs up.*)

ROY. (*Turns back to her.*) Are you *crazy?* What did you say that for? I told you to stall him.

NORMA. I stalled him. You got two minutes. What do you want from me?

ROY. (*Shakes arm at her.*) You always panic. The minute there's a little crisis, you always go to pieces and panic.

NORMA. (*Shaking her arm back at him.*) Don't wave your broken arm at me. Why don't you use it to get your daughter out of the bathroom?

ROY. (*Very angry, kneeling to her on bed.*) I could say something to you now.

NORMA. (*Confronting him, kneels in turn on bed.*) Then why don't you say it?

ROY. Because it would lead to a fight. And I don't want to spoil this day for you. (*He gets up and crosses back to bathroom door.*) Mimsey, this is your father speaking . . . I think you know I'm not a violent man. I can be stern and strict, but I have never once been violent. Except when I'm angry. And I am really angry now, Mimsey. You can ask your mother. (*Moves away so* Norma *can get to door.*)

NORMA. (*Crossing to the bathroom door.*) Mimsey, this is your mother speaking. It's true darling, your father is very angry.

ROY. (*Moving back to door.*) This is your father again, Mimsey. If you have a problem you want to discuss, unlock the door and we'll discuss it. I'm not going to ask you this again, Mimsey. I've reached the end of my patience. I'm gonna count to three . . . and by God, I'm warning you, young lady, by the time I've reached three . . . *this door better be open!* (*Moving away to below the bed.*) All right—One! . . . Two! . . . THREE! (*There is no reply or movement from behind the door.* Roy *helplessly sinks down on the foot of the bed.*) Where did we fail her?

NORMA. (*Crosses to far side of bed, consoling him as she goes, and sits on edge.*) We didn't fail her.

ROY. They're playing "Here Comes the Bride" downstairs and she's barricaded in a toilet, we must have failed her.

NORMA. (*Sighs.*) All right, if it makes you any happier, we failed her.

ROY. You work and you dream and you hope and you save your whole life for this day, and in one click of a door, suddenly everything crumbles. Why? What's the answer?

MORMA. It's not your fault, Roy. Stop blaming yourself.

ROY. I'm not blaming myself. I know *I've* done my best.

NORMA. (*Turns and looks at him.*) What does that mean?

ROY. It means we're not perfect. We make mistakes, we're only human. I've done my best and we've failed her.

NORMA. Meaning *I* didn't do my best?

ROY. (*Turning to her.*) I didn't say that. I don't know what your best is. Only *you* know what your best is. Did you do your best?

NORMA. Yes, I did my best.

ROY. And I did my best.

NORMA. Then we *both* did our best.

ROY. So it's not our fault.

NORMA. That's what I said before.

(*They turn from each other. Then.*)

ROY. (*Softly.*) Unless one of us didn't do our best.
NORMA. (*Jumping up and moving away.*) I don't want to discuss it anymore.
ROY. All right, then what are we going to do?
NORMA. I'm having a heart attack, *you* come up with something.
ROY. How? All right, I'll go down and tell them. (*Gets up and moves to bedroom door.*)
NORMA. (*Moving to door in front of him.*) Tell them? Tell them what?

LAST of the RED HOT LOVERS

Premièred December 28, 1969
at the Eugene O'Neill Theatre, New York City

Directed by Robert Moore

CAST

Barney Cashman	James Coco
Elaine Navazio	Linda Lavin
Bobbi Michele	Marcia Rodd
Jeanette Fisher	Doris Roberts

The action of the play takes place in an apartment in New York's East Thirties.

Barney Cashman is the middle-aged proprietor of a fish restaurant in New York City. He is a devoted husband of twenty-three years, gentle, kind, and decent. His life has been exemplary. But at age forty-seven he has awakened to the fact that his life has also been adventureless and boring. Threatened by thoughts of his mortality, he has decided to break the pattern of his bland existence by having an affair. So he arranges assignations to take place in his mother's apartment while she is away doing volunteer work at Mount Sinai. But each is doomed by character conflicts and the fact that Barney is essentially a moral person, a good man who, in spite of his desperation, is not comfortable with cheating on his wife.

His first encounter is with Elaine Navazio, a tough-talking realist who is no stranger to infidelity. Barney is clumsy and reticent. Elaine is bold and impatient and quickly tires of his furtiveness and inexperience. The second liaison is between Barney and Bobbi Michele, a young, dope-smoking, promiscuous basket case whose incessant ramblings reveal her aberrant lifestyle. The wide moral and generational gap between them results in another failed rendezvous. The final episode involves Jeanette Fisher, a personal friend of Barney and his wife who is morbidly depressed and negative due to her husband's affair. Her depression hangs over the proceedings like a wet shroud, once again dooming the assignation.

From Act I:
Barney—45-50
Elaine—35-45

Barney, using his mother's apartment for a liaison while she's away working at Mount Sinai, is a nervous, bumbling wreck. Elaine, on the other hand, is a seasoned, sardonic realist who quickly tires of his reticent, guilt-riddled behavior.

ELAINE. Is that your wife I see once in a while in the restaurant? The tall blond woman with the mink coat and the space shoes?
BARNEY. That's right. How did you know?
ELAINE. I figured the only person who'd come in and take money out of the cash register and leave without saying a word is either a mute cook or your wife.
BARNEY. She does that once a week. She goes to the bank on Fridays.
ELAINE. (*Nods.*) How long are you and the depositor married?
BARNEY. (*Shrugs.*) A long time.
ELAINE. How long? Five years? Ten years? What?

BARNEY. Twenty-three years.

ELAINE. (*Nods.*) Oh, professionals . . . So here it is Friday, and your wife's at the bank with her space shoes, and your mother's rolling bandages at Mount Sinai . . . and you are all alone with an attractive woman with an empty glass.

BARNEY. (*Takes it.*) Oh, I'm sorry. (*He goes back to the bottle. He surreptitiously smells his fingers and then starts to pour Scotch into her glass.*) You sure you don't want ice?

ELAINE. Positive. You just did it again.

BARNEY. Did what?

ELAINE. Smelled your fingers. That's the third time you smelled your fingers since I'm here.

BARNEY. Did I do that? I wasn't even conscious of it.

ELAINE. Is that an occupational hazard? Owning a fish restaurant and always worrying how your fingers smell?

BARNEY. Well, it's opening those clams and oysters. I enjoy doing it. I do about eight dozen every morning. That's for the last twenty years. I use soap, perfume, aftershave lotion, turpentine . . . They're all right for a few hours, then about four in the afternoon—it comes back in just like the tide.

ELAINE. I wouldn't worry about it if I were you.

BARNEY. Well, it's not the suavest thing in the world. I mean sitting here in a nice blue suit with an attractive woman, smelling my fingers.

ELAINE. The smelly fingers don't bother me as much as the blue suit. You never wear anything else, do you?

BARNEY. Not in the restaurant. My father always taught me, a business man should always wear a dignified blue suit. I wear them in the summer, too, only in a cooler fabric.

ELAINE. Good. I was concerned.

BARNEY. What do they call a person like me? A creature of habit?

ELAINE. Yes, I think that's what they call a person like you. Didn't you ever have a wild, crazy desire for a brown sports jacket?

BARNEY. I have sports jackets in my closet at home. I have a brown sports jacket and a gray checked sports jacket . . .

ELAINE. Is that were you wear them? In your closet at home?

BARNEY. I wear them all the time. I'm not as staid as you think.

ELAINE. Yes, you are. Staid is a very staid word. You own a car?

BARNEY. Yes.

ELAINE. A Buick, right?

BARNEY. My God, how did you know?

ELAINE. (*Shrugs.*) It goes with blue suits.

BARNEY. You're a very unusual woman, Elaine. Like the way you came to my restaurant. I've never seen you before and suddenly you come back for lunch eight days in a row. What is it, a special high-protein diet?

ELAINE. I get cravings.

BARNEY. You mean to eat?

ELAINE. To eat, to touch, to smell, to see, to do . . . A sensual, physical pleasure that can only be satisfied at *that* particular moment.

BARNEY. You mean like after an hour of handball, a cold Pepsi?

ELAINE. (*She looks at him.*) I'm gong to have trouble with you, right? . . . I have a craving for another Scotch.

BARNEY. Coming right up. (*Takes her glass and starts to go over to the bottle, where his hand passes in front of his face.*)

ELAINE. (*Chidingly.*) Eh, eh. Caught you again.

BARNEY. I wasn't smelling my fingers. I was looking at my watch.

ELAINE. Oh. Is it time to smell your fingers yet?

BARNEY. I was just thinking about my mother. We have plenty of time.

ELAINE. What time is it?

BARNEY. Ten after three.

ELAINE. And Mount Sinai lets out at five. We've got an hour and fifty minutes. Okay, you want to make the first move?

From Act II:
Barney—45-50
Bobbi—25-30

Bobbi, an off-the-wall, aspiring young actress, is the antithesis of everything Barney represents and, as a consequence, any connection is impossible. Bobbi's ruminations about her weird friends, tenuous show biz connections and dope smoking life-style unravel Barney and he encourages her early departure.

  But first, Bobbi insists, he must join her in a joint, a first-time experience for the naïve Barney.

BOBBI. (*Opens the box containing her dope.*) I just have to have a few drags before I face the world again.
BARNEY. Now? Now? Wouldn't you be better off facing the world first and then relaxing when you get home?
BOBBI. Doctor's orders.
BARNEY. Well, I wouldn't want you to go without your medicine, but, (*She takes out two sticks.*) as I said before, I'm way behind in this story— (*She holds one out to him.*) What's that?
BOBBI. You said you'd have one with me later.
BARNEY. I said "maybe later." *Maybe . . .*
BOBBI. You said "later."
BARNEY. No, no. I said "maybe later." I remember saying the maybe just before the later. We were talking about that incident in the Mexican hotel.
BOBBI. I think it's very impolite of you. I'm not going unless you have one with me . . . if I have to stay all night.

BARNEY. Two puffs. Two quick puffs and then I really have to get back to work. (*Puts it in his mouth and takes the matches.*)

BOBBI. I like the way you hold it in your mouth. You can tell a lot about a man by the way he holds pot in his mouth.

BARNEY. Here we go. (*Lights both.*)

BOBBI. Good?

BARNEY. Oh, yeah. Mm, man, that's pot.

BOBBI. It's better when you close your eyes.

BARNEY. Oh, listen, don't I know. But I really don't have time to close my eyes. I'm just taking one more puff and then I've got to get to work. (*Takes another quick drag.*) Okay. Finished. Really terrific. My best pot this week. (*Starts to put it out in the ashtray.*)

BOBBI. Let me see you get it in your lungs and hold it there.

BARNEY. You don't want to see that. There's nothing to see. A man with pot in his lungs. You must have seen it a hundred times.

BOBBI. Why won't you inhale it?

BARNEY. I will. I will. Watch. I promise. (*Takes another drag.*)

BOBBI. Swallow it.

BARNEY. Hmm?

BOBBI. Swallow it! (Barney *swallows.*) Okay, now exhale. (Barney *exhales; nothing comes out.*)

BARNEY. Oh, my God, it didn't come out. It's still in there.

BOBBI. In a few minutes you mouth will feel numb and your toes will start to tingle.

BARNEY. Good, good. I can't wait.

BOBBI. What do you feel now?

BARNEY. Outside of sharp pain, nothing very much.

BOBBI. Is your mouth getting dry?

BARNEY. A little. (*Tests his mouth.*) It's drying now. (*Tests it again.*) There it goes, it's all dried up.

BOBBI. This is quality grass. You can tell, can't you? It's from South America.

BARNEY. Well, you know what they say. "You can take pot out of the country, but you can't take the—"

BOBBI. Toes tingling yet?

BARNEY. (*Nods.*) Toes tingling.

BOBBI. Relaxed?

BARNEY. Relaxed. . . Oh, My God, my tongue is paralyzed. I just lost the use of my tongue. I'll never talk again.

BOBBI. You're high, baby, just sit back and enjoy it.

BARNEY. I'll try, I'll try . . . Everything is slowing down. Do you feel everything slowing down?

BOBBI. Mh-hmmm.

BARNEY. (*Puts his hand on his chest.*) Oh, God, I don't feel my heart. What the hell happened to my heart?

BOBBI. Relax . . . Don't fight it, honey.

BOBBI. I'm hanging it out. Here I go. I don't know where I'm going, but I'm going . . .

BOBBI. Just let yourself go.

BARNEY. Oh, boy, what's that? What is that?

BOBBI. What?

BARNEY. I hear my eyes blinking—thump, thump—There it goes again, thump!

BOBBI. If you got it, baby, flaunt it.

BARNEY. I'm flaunting it, I'm flaunting it. (*A big, enormous smile spreads across his face.*) Wheeeee!

BOBBI. God, the things that have happened to me.

BARNEY. I heard, I heard. I can't wait to read the book.

BOBBI. Did I tell you about this man in California?

BARNEY. The dognapper or the teeth sharpener?

BOBBI. Well, I was in love with him. You know about love, I can tell . . . You must have suffered plenty, didn't you?

BARNEY. Many years ago I was involved with an older woman from Newark, New Jersey.

BOBBI. Oh, yeah, I know the scene. How long did it last?

BARNEY. A bout fifteen minutes.

BOBBI. You got to make it alone in this world. All I need is one show. The talent's there, it's just a question of time.

BARNEY. That's all it is, Bob.

BOBBI. People don't want to see you make good . . . they're all jealous . . . they're all rotten . . . they're all vicious.

BARNEY. So many things I wanted to do . . . but I'll never do 'em. So many places I wanted to see . . . I'll never see 'em. Trapped . . . we're all trapped . . . Help! Help!

BOBBI. (*After a moment's quiet she begins to sing.*)

What the world needs now, is love, sweet love.

(Barney *joins her, humming along.*)

That's the only thing that there's just too little of . . .

From Act III:
Barney—45-50
Jeanette—40-50

Jeanette is a close friend of Barney and his wife. She is also proba-bly the singularly most depressed woman in the Western Hemisphere, a prevailing emotional state exacerbated by the fact her husband is having an affair. For this reason she has decided to throw caution to the wind and agree to meet Barney at his mother's apartment. But the affair is doomed due to Jeanett's gloominess and negativity. Why, she won't even put down her purse!

JEANETTE. Barney, do you know I haven't slept with Mel in eight months?

BARNEY. (*That stops him.*) No, I didn't. Eight months, my God. I knew Mel had a bad back but I had no idea—

JEANETTE. *Have not* slept with him in eight months.

BARNEY. Well, listen, Jeanette, that's none of my business. That's between you and Mel . . .

JEANETTE. He's slept with me. I haven't slept with him.

BARNEY. (*Looks at her, puzzled.*) How does that work out?

JEANETTE. I don't particularly enjoy sex, Barney.

BARNEY. Is that right? Ever?

JEANETTE. It was important to me once. Nothing is very important to me any more.

BARNEY. You're just tense, Jeanette. You're going through a dry period right now. Eight months, my God, no wonder . . .

JEANETTE. Has Mel indicated in any way that there was trouble between us?

BARNEY. None. Mel is not a talker.

JEANETTE. I know you see him all the time.

BARNEY. I play handball with him on Saturday mornings. We never discuss personal problems. He serves, I hit it back.

JEANETTE. He didn't seem upset?

BARNEY. No, Can I take your pocketbook, Jeanette?

JEANETTE. *You* wouldn't talk, would you, Barney?

BARNEY. Me, Jeanette? I'm surprised that you would even think—

JEANETTE. Then I don't have to worry about my name ever coming up in a cocktail party—

BARNEY. May God strike me dead! May I never live to see my oldest girl married, if I ever mentioned even casually—

JEANETTE. Swear!

BARNEY. I just swore. May I become totally paralyzed from the hips down—

JEANETTE. It was not easy for me to come here today.

BARNEY. May my hands get crippled with arthritis. I'm surprised that you would even think . . .

JEANETTE. I'm not very good at this sort of thing, Barney.

BARNEY. Who *is,* Jeanette?

JEANETTE. I don't even know what I'm supposed to do.

BARNEY. I'd put my pocketbook down first if I were you . . .

JEANETTE. My only concern is that whatever happens between us will never go beyond these four walls. (*Crosses to window.*)

BARNEY. May my restaurant be destroyed by fire, Jeanette. You'll never have to worry as long as you live. I told you that the other night.

JEANETTE. Did Mel ever mention being involved with another woman?

BARNEY. No.

JEANETTE. Would you tell me if he did?

BARNEY. Yes. Yes, I would tell you.

JEANETTE. You would?

BARNEY. Yes.

JEANETTE. Why would you tell me?

BARNEY. I don't know why. You asked me if I would; I'm trying to be polite, that's all.

JEANETTE. I see.

BARNEY. Can I take your pocketbook, Jeanette?

JEANETTE. What do you think about all this, Barney?

BARNEY. About all what?

JEANETTE. About all this that's going on.

BARNEY. *Nothing's* going on, Jeanette, I can't even get your pocketbook.

JEANETTE. You're not appalled by the times we live in, by all the promiscuity you find everywhere?

BARNEY. I don't find it anywhere. I *hear* a lot about it, I haven't found any. You want to sit down a few minutes? You're here, you might as well sit.

JEANETTE. Let me ask you a question, Barney. Do you have any guilt about asking me here today?

BARNEY. Do I have any guilt?

JEANETTE. Don't repeat the question, just answer it.

BARNEY. What? Do I have any guilt? . . . No, I do not.

JEANETTE. In other words, you don't care who you hurt?

BARNEY. I'm not hurting anymore.

JEANETTE. Really? You want to think about that answer?

BARNEY. Not necessarily . . . Why probe deeply into everything?

JEANETTE. Exactly. That's the attitude we live with today. Don't think about it. Well, I'm not going to think about it, Barney. I'm going to become like everyone else in the world. That's why I'm here today. (*Opens her purse, takes out a pillbox and puts a pill in her mouth.*)

BARNEY. Somehow I think we've gotten off on a tangent, Jeanette . . . What are you doing? What's that?

JEANETTE. Digilene. It's for depression.

THE GINGERBREAD LADY

Premièred December 13, 1970
at the Plymouth Theatre, New York City

Directed by Robert Moore

CAST

Jimmy Perry	Michael Lombard
Manuel	Alex Colon
Toby Landau	Betsy von Furstenberg
Evy Meara	Maureen Stapleton
Polly Meara	Ayn Ruymen
Lou Tanner	Charles Siebert

The action of the play takes place in a brownstone apartment in the West Seventies of New York City.

Evy Meara, an alcoholic, out-of-work nightclub singer, has returned home after a period of rehabilitation. She is a promiscuous, irresponsible, lonely divorcee who has recently been spurned by Lou Tanner, a younger, impoverished musician. Her best friends are Jimmy Perry, a homosexual, unsuccessful actor, and Toby Landau, a very attractive but decidedly superficial individual. The three are kindred spirits—feckless misfits who lean on each other for support and solace. Then into the mix comes Polly, Evy's teenage daughter.

After three weeks, Evy, still weak and delicately balanced, is feeling the strain of Polly's overweening concern. And, on a fateful evening when Jimmy arrives nearly suicidal due to the fact that he has lost the part in a new play, and Toby arrives shattered because her husband has just announced his plans to divorce, Evy loses herself in a tailspin of drunkenness and engages in insults that alienate those she loves.

After an alcoholic night with Lou Tanner, during which he brutalizes her, Evy returns to be lectured by Toby, who admonishes her for her lifestyle and begs her to release Polly before she is corrupted. And she makes the attempt. But Polly, displaying maturity and grit, refuses to abandon her mother. The play ends on an upbeat note of hope and optimism.

From Act I:
Toby and Evy—40-45

Evy has just been returned to her apartment by Toby (her beautiful but self-possessed friend) after ten weeks of alcohol rehabilitation and is greeted by Jimmy who has been looking after her flat during her absence.

After Jimmy has gone to the kitchen to prepare a sandwich for Evy:

TOBY. (*Looking at herself in mirror.*) And what can I do, Evy?
EVY. You can stop looking at yourself and give me a cigarette.
TOBY. You *are* nervous, aren't you?
EVY. I hated that place so much I used to save up matches planning to burn it down. It was a Goddamn prison. And then when it came time to leave I was afraid to go . . . I suddenly felt comfortable there . . . Can I have a cigarette, please?

TOBY. That's almost a whole pack since we left the hospital. Are you sure they said it was all right to smoke?

EVY. Once you pay your bill and check out, they don't care if you get knocked up by a dwarf. (*Takes cigarette and smokes.*) I thought I'd have a million things to do when I got home. I'm here six minutes, I'm bored to death.

TOBY. You're got to give yourself time, Evy. And then you're going to start your life all over again and you're going to grow up to be a beautiful wonderful person like me.

EVY. What's that? What's the crap you're putting on your face?

TOBY. It's special crap that protects the skin. Have you noticed you've never seen pores on me. As long as you've known me, have you ever seen a single pore on my face?

EVY. I've never seen your face . . . Who are you anyway?

TOBY. A woman can never be too pretty. It's her feminine obligation. I love my looks, don't you?

EVY. You're gorgeous. If you went bald and lost your teeth, you'd still be cute looking. Leave yourself alone.

TOBY. I can't. Isn't it terrible? I'm obsessed.

EVY. You remind me of the psycho in the room next to me. She used to shampoo her eyelashes every night. Thought all the doctors were in love with her. And eighty-seven-year-old virgin screwball.

TOBBY. What a sweet story. You just going to sit there forever? Aren't you going to unpack or something?

EVY. Unpack what? A pair of pajamas and a bottle of mineral oil? Besides, I'm never going in that bedroom again. I ruined half my life in there, the next half I'm playing it safe.

TOBY. I understand perfectly. But how will you get to the bathroom?

EVY. Over the roof and down the pipes. Just worry about your face, all right?

TOBY. I can worry about both. I wish I could stay with you tonight.

EVY. Then why don't you stay with me tonight?

TOBY. I have to meet Martin at Pavilion for dinner. It's business. I distract the client.

EVY. Some friend you are.

TOBY. Don't say it like that. I'm a wonderful friend. I'm sensitive. You want me to be hurt?

EVY. Don't pout. You'll crack your makeup and start an avalanche on your face.

From Act I:
Jimmy and Evy—40-45

The Cuban delivery boy has just departed and Jimmy, Evy's homosexual, out-of-work actor friend, is upset by Evy's apparent acceptance of his brashness and innuendo. But Jimmy is a true, caring friend.

JIMMY. (*Yells.*) Jesus Christ! Why didn't you invite him in to listen to your Xaiver Cugat records? Are you crazy?

EVY. Oh, come on, he's delivery boy.

JIMMY. I saw the look he gave you and I know what he wants to deliver.

EVY. I'm not in that kind of trouble yet . . . Maybe in a few weeks, but not yet.

JIMMY. I can't trust you. I can't trust you alone for ten minutes.

EVY. I can be trusted for ten minutes.

JIMMY. I know you, Evy. I wouldn't leave you with the Pope during Holy Week . . . Haven't you had enough trouble this year?

EVY. I've had enough for the rest of my life. For Christ's sake, I'm not going to shack up with a delivery boy. I don't even have a quarter to give him a tip.

JIMMY. You'll charge it like everything else.

EVY. Oh, God, Jimmy, I really love you. You don't know how good it is to have somebody worried about you.

JIMMY. Well, I hate it. I have enough trouble worrying about me. I'm forty years old and I can't get a job without clothes anymore. If you want to carry on with Pancho Gonzales, that's up to you.

EVY. (*Puts arms around* Jimmy.) . . . Of all the stinking people in this world, you sure aren't one of them.

JIMMY. Well, I'm glad you finally realize all the others are stinking.

EVY. Why don't you marry me?

JIMMY. Because you're a drunken nymphomaniac and I'm a homosexual. We'd have trouble getting our kids into a good school.

EVY. Give me a kiss. (*He kisses her lightly.*) Come on. Give me a real kiss. Who the hell's gonna know. (*He kisses her with feeling.*)

JIMMY. God will punish us for the terrible thing we're doing.

EVY. Don't get depressed, but you get me very excited.

JIMMY. I don't have to say and listen to this kinds of talk. (*Breaks away from her.*) I've got to go. If you promise to behave yourself, I may be nice to you when I'm a star.

EVY. We could live together in Canada. They don't do sex in Canada.

JIMMY. (*Putting on his bag.*) Stop it, Evy, you're confusing my hormones. I'm late.

EVY. Jimmy!

JIMMY. (*Stops.*) What?

EVY. Nothing. I just love you and want to thank you for being here today.

JIMMY. Don't thank me, just pray for me. Pray that I get this show because I think it's the last one in the world.

EVY. Will you call me the minute you hear anything?

JIMMY. It's off-Broadway, there are no phones. (*On his way out.*) I bought you that Stouffers macaroni that you love. And some Sara

Lee cheesecake. And I made you enough coffee until Friday . . . Will you remember to drink it?

EVY. Drinking is one thing I remember.

JIMMY. And get some sleep.

EVY. I promise.

JIMMY. And if Jose Ferrer shows his face again, don't open the door. The only groceries he's bringing next time are his own. (*Exits, closing the door behind him.*)

From Act I:
Polly—17
Evy—40-45

Polly, Evy's teenage daughter, has arrived and announced her plans to stay. Evy is reluctant and argues against her moving in, but Polly, a concerned and loving child, is firm in her commitment to stay.

(Evy *who has phoned Polly, terminates the call when the girl enters, suitcase in hand.*)

(*Into phone.*) Never mind, I just heard from her. (*Hangs up and stares at* Polly.)

POLLY. I don't want to get your hopes up, but I have reason to believe I'm your daughter!

EVY. No, you're not. My daughter would have called first.
. . . (*No longer able to contain herself.*) You rotten kid, you want to give me a heart attack? (*They rush to each other, arms around each other in a huge, warm embrace.* Evy *Squeezes her tightly.*) Oh, God, Polly, Polly . . .

POLLY. I was hoping I'd get here before you. But I was late getting out of school. Of all the damn days . . . (*They break the embrace.* Evy *wipes her eyes.*)

EVY. Okay, I'm crying. You satisfied? You just destroyed a helpless woman . . . Well, why the hell aren't you crying?

POLLY. I'm too happy. I can't believe it. My God, look at you.

EVY. What do you think?

POLLY. You're gorgeous. Skinniest mother I ever had. I can wear your clothes now.

EVY. What size dress do you wear?

POLLY. Five.

EVY. Tough, kid, I wear four. (*Wipes teary eyes again.*) Damn, I knew this would happen. You weren't supposed to know I was home. I needed three days before I could face you.

POLLY. I called the hospital this morning. You didn't think I could wait, did you?

EVY. Neither could I. Oh, God, give me another hug, I can't stand it. (*They embrace.*) All right, if we're going to get physical, let's close the door. There's enough talk about me in this building. (*Closes the door.* Polly *crosses and gets the suitcase out of the doorway.*)

POLLY. I'll get that. (*Picks it up.*)

EVY. Have you had dinner yet?

POLLY. I haven't even had lunch. I was too nervous.

EVY. I just loaded up for the winter. We'll have a food festival. Come on, take your coat off, let me look at you. Hey, what'd you do with your hair?

POLLY. Nothing.

EVY. I know. It's been three months, when you gonna do something?

POLLY. Don't bug me about the way I look. I'm not secure yet. (*Picks up suitcase, heads for bedroom.*)

EVY. I should have your problem. Where you going with that?

POLLY. In the bedroom.

EVY. What is it?

POLLY. (*Looks at it.*) Looks like a suitcase.

EVY. Thanks, I was wondering. What's in the suitcase?

POLLY. (*Shrugs.*) Dresses, shoes, books, things like that.

EVY. Why do you have things like that in your suitcase?

POLLY. Well, otherwise they fall on the floor.

EVY. All right, no one likes a smartass for a daughter. What's going on here?

POLLY. Nothing's going on. Can't I stay?

EVY. Tonight? You know you can.

POLLY. Okay. I'm staying tonight. (*Starts for bedroom again.*)

EVY. With all that? You must be some heavy sleeper.

POLLY. Okay, *two* nights, let's not haggle.

EVY. Hey, hey, just a minute. Put the suitcase down. (Polly *looks at her. She puts it down.*) . . . Now look at me.

POLLY. I'm looking.

EVY. And I know what you're thinking. Oh, no, you don't.

POLLY. Why not?

EVY. Because I don't need roommates, thank you . . . If you had a beard, it would be different.

POLLY. I don't want to be your roommate, I just want to live with you.

EVY. You lonely? I'll send you to camp. You have a home, what are you bothering me for?

POLLY. You can't throw me out, I'm your flesh and blood.

EVY. I just got rid of my flesh. I'm not sentimental.

POLLY. I've already decided I'm moving in, you have nothing to say about it.

EVY. In the first place, you're not allowed to live here. It's not up to you or me.

POLLY. And in the second place?

EVY. I don't need a second place. The first one wiped us out. You live where your father tells you to live.

POLLY. Exactly. Where do I put the suitcase?

EVY. Are you telling me *your* father gave you permission to move in here with me?

POLLY. Right.

EVY. *Your* father?

POLLY. That's the one.

EVY. A tall man. Grayish hair, wears blue suits, spits a little when he talks?

POLLY. Would you like to speak with him yourself?

EVY. Not sober, I don't. What does your stepmother think about this? What's her name, Lucretia?

POLLY. Felicia.

EVY. Felicia, some name. He must spit pretty good when he says that. Did she ever get that clicking in her teeth fixed?

POLLY. Nope. Still clicking.

EVY. That's a nice way to live, with a spitter and a clicker. Thank God he didn't get custody of me too.

POLLY. That's why I'm begging you to take me in. I can't do my homework with all that noise.

EVY. God's truth, Polly? He really said yes?

POLLY. He likes me. He wouldn't kid around with my life.

EVY. Why don't I believe it?

POLLY. We've been talking about it for months. He knows how hard you've been trying, he spoke to your doctor, he knows you're all right . . . And he thinks that you need me now.

EVY. *Now* I need you? Where does he think I've been the last seven years, Guatemala?

POLLY. He knows where you're been.

EVY. And what about you? Is this what you really want?

POLLY. I've been packed for three years. Every June I put in bigger sizes.

EVY. You wanna hear something? My whole body is shaking. My whole body is shaking. I'm scared stiff. I wouldn't know the first thing about taking care of you.

POLLY. I'm seventeen years old. How hard could it be?

EVY. I'll level with you, it's not the best thing I do. I was feeling very motherly one time, I bought a couple of turtles, two for eighty-five cents, Irving and Sam. I fed them once. In the morning they were floating on their backs. I don't think I could go through that again.

POLLY. I'm a terrific swimmer.

EVY. Jesus, the one thing I hoped I wouldn't have is a dumb daughter. What kind of influence would I be on you? I talk filthy. I have always talked filthy. I'm a congenital filthy talker.

POLLY. Son of a bitch.

EVY. I don't think that's funny.

POLLY. Well, I just got here, give me a chance.

From Act III:
Toby and Evy—40-45

A series of chaotic events resulted in the fragile Evy lapsing into a drunken tirade followed by a destructive night with a former lover. Here she is confronted by Toby the morning after:

TOBY. Well, good morning.

EVY. That's entirely possible.

TOBY. Do you know what time it is?

EVY. November?

TOBY. Evy!

EVY. Later, Toby, I have to go to the john.

TOBY. I refuse to talk to your unbrushed hair all morning. Turn around and look at me. (*Evy turns around revealing a black-and-blue eye.*) Oh, God . . . your eye, Evy, what have you done?

EVY. You want to be my friend, Toby, no questions and no sympathy. I'm all right.

TOBY. I don't think I *want* to hear about it.

EVY. Where's Polly?

TOBY. She's been up all night calling everyone. I made her go home and lie down.

EVY. Well, if she sleeps for three weeks I may get away with it.

TOBY. You don't seem to be acting much like a woman who just got beaten up.

EVY. I didn't get beaten up, Toby, just punched. One clean, little punch, I never felt it.

TOBY. Really? Have you seen what you look like?

EVY. Compared to you, what difference does it make? . . . I'm all right, I promise you.

TOBY. Sit down, let me put some ice on it.

EVY. I've already had medical attention. A dog licked my face while I was down.

TOBY. Who did it?

EVY. What difference does it make?

TOBY. Because I feel responsible.

EVY. Come on, Toby. I got what I asked for last night because I wasn't getting anything else. (*Sits.*) All right, I'm sitting. Are you happy now?

TOBY. How can I be happy when your face is half smashed in? How many places did you have to go before you found what you were looking for?

EVY. Just one. If there's one thing I know how to do, it's shop.

TOBY. (*Turns away.*) Oh, Christ, sometimes you disgust me.

EVY. That seems to be the general feeling around town.

TOBY. It was Lou Tanner, wasn't it?

EVY. That's him. The man I love.

TOBY. Jesus, I knew it. There was always something about him that frightened me. You could see it in his eyes.

EVY. Never mind the eyes, it's his big fist you gotta watch . . . I wouldn't hate you if you left me alone now, Toby.

TOBY. Why did you go there, Evy?

EVY. He plays requests, I was lonesome.

TOBY. Why did you start drinking yesterday? Everything was going so good for you. Why, Evy?

EVY. What do you want, a nice, simple answer? When I was six years old my father didn't take me to the circus . . .How the hell do I know why I do anything?

TOBY. Didn't you learn anything in the ten weeks at the hospital?

EVY. The doctor tried to explain but I was too busy making a pass at him . . . If I knew, Toby, would it make any difference?

TOBY. It would help.

EVY. If you haven't eaten in three months you don't want a description of food, you want a little hot something in the plate.

TOBY. And did you get your fill last night, Evy? Did you get your little hot something in the plate?

EVY. No, but we negotiated for a while . . .

TOBY. With someone like that? A deadbeat musician who doesn't give a damn about hitting some drunken woman.

EVY. You just don't get hit like that, you gotta ask for it . . . I happened to make a bad choice. I broke his guitar. I smashed it against the refrigerator, handed him the pieces and said, "Now you can look for work you're equipped to do." I thought it was cute, the man has no sense of humor.

TOBY. The truth, Evy. When he was beating you, did you enjoy it?

EVY. Well, for a second there I said to myself, it hurts like hell—but it sure beats indifference. (*Gets up.*) Is there anything in the kitchen? I'm always hungry after a fight.

THE PRISONER of SECOND AVENUE
(L)

Premièred November 11, 1971
at the Eugene O'Neill Theatre, New York City.

CAST

Mel Edison	Peter Falk
Edna Edison	Lee Grant
Harry Edison	Vincent Gardenia
Pearl	Florence Stanley
Jessie	Tresa Hughes
Pauline	Dena Dietrich

The action of the play takes place in the Edison's 14th floor apartment on New York's East Side.

The pressures of urban life are getting to Mel Edison, an account executive with a New York advertising agency. His apartment is noisy and poorly maintained, crime is rampant, air and noise pollution is unbearable, the city is filthy, and after twenty-two years he is afraid of losing his job. He is tense, anxious, and suffering from insomnia. Then his apartment is literally cleaned out by thieves. They even take the Valium! To further complicate matters, his worst fears are then realized when he is fired. As a final blow to his dignity, he is doused with water by his upstairs neighbor, an act that solidifies his negative feelings regarding the sad state of humankind. Like a loyal soldier, wife Edna takes a job as a secretary to tide them over until Mel finds work. But his job-hunting efforts prove futile and he becomes a depressed recluse, climbing the walls of his apartment. Humiliated at living off Edna's income, his feeling of self-worth shattered, Mel lapses into a state of deep depression, extreme paranoia, and a burning need to retaliate against the water-dumper upstairs—at the first snowfall he plans to bury the son of a bitch as he enters the building below. He suffers a breakdown, which requires sedation and psychiatric care.

Mel's older brother, Harry, and his two sisters, in an apparent act of family caring, come to offer help. But the underlying reality of costs results in bickering, discord, and disagreement, and Edna spurns them for their lack of true compassion.

After several weeks of therapy, Mel, greatly improved, realizes that Edna is showing symptoms he had experienced as a result of workplace pressures. And, when she informs him that she, too, is out of work because of business failure, he is positive, contained, and supportive, further testimony to the fact that he is mentally stable. When brother Harry arrives with a no-strings-attached check for twenty-five thousand dollars, Mel is touched but rejects his offer. Mel, during a touching exchange, learns that Harry, a successful businessman, has never felt loved, and that he has always envied Mel as family favorite.

At play's end, heavy snow begins to fall on the city. Mel goes to a closet and removes a snow shovel he has reserved for the purpose of getting revenge on the son of a bitch above. He and Edna represent a picture of solidarity, committed to braving whatever the future holds.

From Act I, scene ii:
Edna and Mel—40-45

New York is a mess. Its crime, pollution, over-crowding, and a total lack of civility have driven Mel up the wall. Now—compounding the tension and contributing to the slow unraveling of his fragile nerves—his apartment has been literally cleaned out by thieves (they've even taken the dental floss) and he has been fired from his ad agency job.

EDNA. Nobody steals dental floss and mouth wash. Only sick people. Only that's who live in the world today. SICK, SICK, SICK PEOPLE! (*She sits, wrung out emotionally.* Mel *crosses to her, puts his arm on her shoulder, comforting her.*)

MEL . . . It's all right . . . It's all right, Edna . . . (*He looks through papers on table.*)

EDNA. Can you imagine if I walked in and found them here? What would I have done, Mel?

MEL. You were very lucky, Edna. Very lucky.

EDNA. But what would I have done?

MEL. What's the difference? You didn't walk in and find them.

EDNA. But supposing I did? What would I have done?

MEL. You'd say, "Excuse me," close the door and come back later. What would you do, sit and watch? Why do you ask me such questions? It didn't happen, did it?

EDNA. It *almost* happened. If I walked in her five minutes sooner.

MEL. (*Walking away from her.*) You couldn't have been gone only five minutes . . . It took the Santini Brothers two days to move everything in, three junkies aren't gonna move it all out in five minutes.

EDNA. Seven minutes, eight minutes, what's the difference?

MEL. (*Opens the door, looks at lock.*) The lock isn't broken, it's just jimmied. I don't even know how they got in here.

EDNA. Maybe they found my key in the street.

MEL. (*Closes door. Looks at her.*) What do you mean, found your key? Don't you have your key?

EDNA. No, I lost it. I thought it was somewhere in the house, maybe I lost it in the street.

MEL. If you didn't have you key. How were you going to get back in the house when you went shopping?

EDNA. I left the door open.

MEL. You-left-the-door-open?

EDNA. I didn't have a key, how was I going to get back into the house?

MEL. *So you left the door open?* In a city with the highest crime rate in the history of the wold, *you left the door open?*

EDNA. What was I going to do? Take the furniture with me? I was only gone five minutes. How did they know I was going to leave the door open?

MEL. They know! They know! A door opens, it doesn't lock, the whole junkie world lights up. "Door open, 14th floor, 88th Street and Second Avenue." They know!

EDNA. They don't know anything. They have to go around trying doors.

MEL. And what did you think? They were going to try every door in this house except yours? "Let's leave 14A alone, fellas, it looks like a nice door."

EDNA. If they're going to go around trying doors, they have twenty-three hours and fifty-five minutes a day to try them. I didn't think they would try ours the five minutes I was out of the house. I gambled! I lost!

MEL. What kind of gamble is that to take? If you lose, they get everything. If you win, they rob somebody else.

EDNA. I *had* to shop. There was nothing in the house to eat tonight.

MEL. All right, now you have something to eat and nothing to eat it with . . . Why didn't you call up and have them send in?

EDNA. Because I shop in a cheap store that doesn't deliver. I am trying to save us money because you got me so worried the other night. I was just trying to save us money . . . Look how much money I saved us. (Edna *starts to pick up things.*)

MEL. . . . What are you doing?

EDNA. We can't leave everything like this. I want to clean up.

MEL. Now?

EDNA. The place is a mess. We have people coming over in a few minutes.

MEL. The *police?* You want the place to look nice for the police?. . . You're worried they're going to put it down in their books. "Bad Housekeeper?" . . . Leave it alone. Maybe they'll find some clues.

EDNA. I can't find out what's missing until I put everything back in its place.

MEL. What do you mean? You know what's missing. The television, the liquor, the kitchen money, the medicine chest and the Hi-Fi . . . That's it, isn't it? *(Pause.)* Isn't it? (Edna *looks away.*) . . . Okay, what did they get?

EDNA. Am I a detective? Look, you'll find out. (*He glares at her, looks around the room, doesn't know where to begin. He decides to check the bedroom. He storms down the hall and disappears. Edna, knowing what soon to expect, sits on a chair in the dining area and stares out the window. She takes out a hanky and wipes some dirt from the windowsill.* Mel *returns. Calmly. At least outwardly calm. He takes a deep breath.*)

MEL. . . . Where are my suits?

EDNA. They were there this morning. They're not there now. They must have taken your suits.

MEL. (*Still trying to be calm.*) Seven suits? Three sports jackets? Eight pairs of slacks?

EDNA. If that's what you had, that's what they got.

MEL. I'm lucky my tuxedo is in the cleaners.

EDNA. (*Still staring out window.*) They sent it back this morning.

MEL. . . . Well, they did a good job of it . . . Cleaned me out . . . Left a pair of khaki pants and my golf hat . . . Anybody asks us out to dinner this week, ask them if it's all right if I wear khaki pants and a golf hat. DIRTY BASTARDS! (*In what can only be described as an insane tantrum, he picks up ashtrays from the sideboard and throws them to the floor of the kitchen . . . Uncontrollably until all his energy and his vitriol have been exhausted . . . he stands there panting.*)

EDNA. . . . It's just things, Mel. Just some old suits and coats, we can replace them. We'll buy new ones. Can't we, Mel?

MEL. With what? . . . *With What?* They *fired* me. (*He sits, back to wall.*)

EDNA. Oh, my God. Don't tell me.

From Act II, scene ii:
Jessie, Pearl, Pauline, and Harry—55-60

While Edna is in the bedroom talking on the phone, Mel's older brother and sisters wait in the front room. They have come with good intentions—to lend financial assistance during Mel's period of rehabilitation. Their conversation is banal, discordant, and typically familial.

(*The women are well-dressed. Two are on a sofa, one sits in an arm chair.* Pauline *is doing needlepoint. Mel is standing. He wears an expensive business suit. He is looking out the window. A pot of coffee and cups are in front of the women on table.*)

JESSIE. He was always nervous.

PEARL. Always.

JESSIE. As far back as I can remember, he was nervous. Never sat still for a minute, always jumpinmg up and down. Am I lying, Pearl?

PEARL. We're his own sisters, who should know better? Up and down, up and down . . . You want some coffee, Harry? Take some coffee.

HARRY. I don't drink coffee.

JESSIE. He always used to fidget. Talked a mile a minute . . . He even chewed his food fast . . . remember how fast he used to chew?

PEARL. Wasn't I there? Didn't I see him chew? I remember . . . Harry, why don't you take some coffee?

HARRY. When did you ever see me drink coffee? You're my sister fifty-three years, you never saw me drink coffee. Why would I drink coffee now?

PEARL. What do I see you, two times a year? I thought maybe you took up coffee.

PAULINE. He wasn't nervous, he was high strung. Melvin was high strung.

PEARL. I call it nervous. As a baby he was nervous, as a boy he was nervous, in the Army he was nervous. How long did he last in the Army, anyway?

JESSIE. Two weeks.

PEARL. There you are. He was nervous.

PAULINE. Where do you think nerves come from. From being high strung.

PEARL. Then why aren't any of us high strung? We all had the same parents. He was nervous, he was fidgety, he chewed fast . . . I never saw him swallow.

JESSIE. No one could talk to him? Poppa could never talk to him, I remember.

PAULINE. How could Poppa talk to him? Mel was three years old when Poppa died.

PEARL. If he wasn't so nervous, Poppa could have talked to him.

HARRY. I never drank coffee in my life. It's poison. Goes right through the system. (*Looks towards bedroom.*) Who's she on the phone with in there anyway?

PEARL. He had the same thing in high school. A nervous breakdown. Remember when he had the nervous breakdown in high school?

HARRY. (*Turns to her.*) Who you talking about?

PEARL. Mel! He had a nervous breakdown in high school. You don't remember?

HARRY. What are you talking about? He didn't have a nervous breakdown, he had a broken arm. He fell in the gym and broke his arm.

PEARL. I'm not talking about that time.

HARRY. And once on his bicycle he broke a tooth.

PEARL. I'm not taking about that time.

HARRY. Then what are you talking about?

PEARL. I'm talking about the time he had a nervous breakdown in high school. I remember it like it was yesterday, don't tell me. Pauline, tell him.

PAULINE. Mel never had a nervous breakdown.

PEARL. Isn't that funny, I thought he had a nervous breakdown. Maybe I'm thinking of somebody else.

HARRY. You can't even remember that I don't drink coffee.

PAULINE. He must have had some terrible experiences in the Army.

HARRY. In two weeks? He wasn't there long enough to get a uniform. None of you know what you're talking about. There was never anything wrong with Mel. Never. His trouble was you babied him too much. All of you.

JESSIE. Why shouldn't we baby him? He was the baby, wasn't he?

HARRY. You babied him, that's his trouble. He never had the responsibilities as a child like I did. That's why he can't handle problems. That's why her flares up. He's a child, an infant.

PEARL. What if I put some milk in the coffee?

HARRY. I DON'T WANT ANY COFFEE!

JESSIE. He doesn't want any coffee, leave him alone.

PAULINE. Correct me if I'm wrong, but when Mel was a tiny baby, didn't you think his head was too large for his body?

PEARL. Mel? Mel had a beautiful head.

PAULINE. I didn't say his head wasn't beautiful. I said it was too large for his body. It always kept falling over to one side. (*She demonstrates.*)

PEARL. All babies heads fall to one side. (*She demonstrates.*)

PAULINE. I know that, but he had trouble getting his up again. (*She demonstrates.*)

HARRY. . . . I was never babied. Poppa wouldn't allow it . . . I was never kissed from the time I was seven years old . . .

JESSIE. Certainly you were kissed.

HARRY. Never kissed . . . I didn't need kissing. The whole world kissed Mel, look where he is today. Who's she talking to in there all this time?

PEARL. . . . Remember the summer he ran away?

PAULINE. He didn't run away for the whole summer. He ran away for one night.

PEARL. Who said he ran away for the whole summer?

PAULINE. Who said it? You said it. You just said, "Remember the summer he ran away."

PEARL. So? He ran away for *one* night for *one* summer.

PAULINE. But you should say it that way. Say, "Remember the summer he ran away for one night?" Don't make it sound like he ran away for the whole summer. That crazy he never was.

PEARL. Did I say Mel was crazy? Who heard me mention the word crazy? Jessie, did you hear crazy from me?

JESSSIE. I heard "crazy" but I wasn't looking where it came from.

THE SUNSHINE BOYS
(V L)

Premièred on December 20, 1972
at the Broadhurst Theatre, New York City

Directed by Alan Arkin

CAST

Willie Clark	Jack Albertson
Ben Silverman	Lewis J. Stadlen
Al Lewis	Sam Levene
Patient	Joe Young
Eddie	John Batiste
Nurse	Lee Meredith
Registered Nurse	Minnie Gentry

The action of the play takes place in an apartment-hotel on upper Broadway.

Willie Clark, one half of the old comedy team Lewis and Clark, is a cantankerous old vaudevillian living alone in a dilapidated New York hotel. His nephew/agent, Ben, looks after him and unsuccessfully attempts to find work for his acerbic, doddering uncle, who still has designs on show business. Al Lewis, a mild-mannered sort, is now retired and lives with his daughter and son-in-law in New Jersey. Willie, embittered because Al broke up their act to become a stock broker, has not spoken to him for eleven years.

After much cajoling, Ben is successful in getting the old partners to recreate their famous comedy sketch for CBS television. During a dress rehearsal at the CBS, old wounds are opened, an argument ensues, and Al walks off the set. Willie, who has worked himself into a lather, collapses with a heart attack.

Recuperating in his hotel room, Willie is still the caustic old show-biz warrior. But Ben tells him that his active entertainment days are over and convinces him to move into the Actors Home in New Brunswick. He also tells him that Al Lewis is in the lobby, is greatly concerned, and wants to pay his respects. Grudgingly, Willie agrees to receive him.

Willie is imperious and insulting and there is nearly another split, but under the acid veneer, it's apparent that there's warmth for his old partner. Willie tells Al affectionately that he is a pain in the ass, but a funny man, and, in a ironic twist, Al informs Willie that he is going to be moving into the Actors Home in New Brunswick. The play ends with the old troupers recalling the halcyon days of vaudeville.

From Act I, scene ii:
Al and Willie—70s

After many years of separation, Willie's nephew has convinced the boys they should put their differences to rest in order to perform their famous "Doctor Sketch" for CBS TV. But old bitterness runs deep, and during their first rehearsal at Willie's hotel, Willie's curmudgeonly behavior and Al's intractability lead to unproductive acrimony.

We pick up with an escalating debate over "Enter" or "Come in:"

AL. You want to stand here and insult me or do you wanna rehearse the sketch?

WILLIE. I would like to do both but we ain't got the time . . . Let's forget the door. Stand in here and say "knock, knock, knock."

AL. (*Comes in and closes the door. Sarcastically.*) I hope I can get out again.

WILLIE. I hope so too . . . (*He places hands behind back and paces.*) Alright, "Knock knock knock."

AL. (*Pantomimes with fist.*) Knock knock knock.

WILLIE. (*Sing-song.*) Enter!

AL. (*Stops, looks at him.*) What do you mean, "Enter?"(*He does it in the same sing-song way.*) What happened to "Come-in?"

WILLIE. It's the same thing, isn't it? Enter or come-in. What's the difference, as long as your in.

AL. The difference is we've done this sketch 12,000 times and you've always said "Come-in" and suddenly today it's "Enter." Why today, after all these years do you suddenly change it to "Enter?"

WILLIE. (*Shrugs.*) I'm trying to freshen up the act.

AL. Who asked you to freshen up the act? They asked for the Doctor Sketch, didn't they? The Doctor Sketch starts with "Come-in" not "Enter." You wanna freshen up something, put some flowers in here.

WILLIE. It's a new generation today. This is not 1934, you know.

AL. No kidding? I didn't get today's paper.

WILLIE. What's bad about "Enter" instead of "Come-in?"

AL. Because it's different. You know why we've been doing it the same way for 43 years? Because it's good.

WILLIE. And do you know why we don't do it anymore? Because we've been doing it the same way for 43 years.

AL. So, if we're not doing it anymore, why are we changing it?

WILLIE. Can I make a comment. Nothing personal? I think you been sitting on a New Jersey porch too long.

AL. What does that mean?

WILLIE. That means I think you been sitting on a New Jersey porch too long. From my window, I see everything that goes on in the world. I see people, I see young people, nice people, bad people, I see holdups, drug addicts, ambulances, car crashes, jumpers from buildings, I see everything. You see a lawnmower and a milkman.

AL. (*Looks at him long.*) And that's why you want to say "Enter" instead of "Come-in?"

WILLIE. Are you listening to me?

AL. (*Looks around.*) Why, there's someone else in the room?

WILLIE. You don't know the first thing that's going on today.

AL. Alright, what's going on today?

WILLIE. Did you ever hear the expression, "That's where it is?" Well, this is where it is and that's where I am.

AL. I see . . . Did you ever hear the expression, "You don't know what the hell you're talking about?" It comes right in front of the other expression, "You *never* know what the hell you're talking about."

WILLIE. *I* wasn't the one who retired. You know why you retired? Because you were tired. You were getting old-fashioned. I was still new-fashioned and I'll *always* be.

AL. I see. That's why you're in such demand. That's why you're such "hot" property today. That's why you do movies you don't do, that's why you're in musicals you're not in, and that's why you make commercials you don't make because you can't even remember to *make* them.

WILLIE. You know what I *do* remember? I remember what a pain in the ass you are to work with, that's what I remember.

AL. That's right. And when you worked with this pain in the ass, you lived in a *five* room suite. Now you live in a *one* room suite . . . And you're still wearing the same God damn pajamas you wore in the five room suite.

WILLIE. I don't have to take this crap from you.

AL. You're lucky you're getting it. No one else want's to give it to you.

WILLIE. I don't want to argue with you. After you say "Knock knock knock" I'm saying "Enter" and if you don't like it, you don't have to come in.

AL. You can't say nothing without my permission. I own fifty per cent of this act.

WILLIE. Then say *your* fifty percent. I'm saying "Enter" in my fifty percent.

AL. If you say "Enter" after "Knock knock knock" . . . I'm coming in alright. But not alone. I'm bringing a lawyer with me

WILLIE. Where? From New Jersey? You're lucky if a *cow* comes with you.

AL. Against *you* in court, I could win with a *cow*. (*He enunciates each point by poking* Willie *in the chest.*)

WILLIE. (*Slaps his hand away.*) The finger? You're starting with the finger again? (*He runs into the kitchen, comes out brandishing a knife.*)

AL. I'll tell you the truth now. I didn't retire. I *escaped.*

Willie. (*Wielding knife.*) The next time you give me the finger, say goodbye to the finger.

AL. (*Hiding behind chair.*) Listen, I got a terrific idea. Instead of working together again, let's never work together again, You're crazy.

WILLIE. I'm crazy, heh? I'M CRAZY!

AL. Keep saying it until you believe it.

WILLIE. I may be crazy, but you're *senile!* You know what that is?

AL. I'm not giving you any straight lines.

WILLIE. Crazy is when you got a couple of parts that go wrong. Senile is when you went the hell out of business. That's you, Mister. (*The phone rings.* Al *moves towards phone.*) Get away from that phone. (*He drives knife into table. Al backs away in shock. Picks up phone.*) Hello?

AL. Is that my daughter?

WILLIE. Hello. How are you?

AL. Is that my daughter? Is that her?

WILLIE. (*Speaks to* Al.) Will you shut up? Will you be quiet? Can't you see I'm talking? Don't you see me on the phone with a person? For God's sakes, behave like a human being for five seconds, will you? . . . WILL YOU BEHAVE FOR FIVE SCEONDS LIKE A HUMAN BEING? (*Into the phone.*) Hello? . . . Yes . . . Just a minute. (*To* Al.) It's your daughter. (*He sits, opens up* Variety.)

AL. (*He takes the phone, turns his back to* Willie, *speaks low.*) Hello . . . Hello, sweetheart . . . No . . . No . . . I can't talk now . . . I said I can't talk now . . . Because he's crazy as a bedbug, that's why.

WILLIE. (*Jumps up.*) Mister is no good but bedbug is alright? (*Yells into phone.*) You father is sick! Come and get your sick father!

AL. (*Turns to him.*) Don't you see me on the phone with a person? Will you please be quiet, for God's sakes! (*Back into phone.*) Listen, I want you to pick me up now . . . I don't want to discuss it, pick me up now. In front of the hotel. Don't park to close, it's filthy here . . . I know what I promised. Don't argue with me. I'm putting on my coat, I'll wait in the street, I'll probably get mugged . . . Alright, just a minute. (*He hands the phone to* Willie.) She'd like to talk to you for a second.

WILLIE. Who is it?

AL. (*Glares at him.*) Mrs. Eleanor Roosevelt . . .What do you mean, who is it? Didn't you just say it's your daughter?

WILLIE. I know it's your daughter. I forgot her name.

AL. Doris.

WILLIE. What does she want?

AL. (*Yells.*) Am I Doris? She'll tell you.

WILLIE. (*He takes phone.*) Hello? . . . Hello, dear, this is Willie Clark . . . Unpleasantness? There was no unpleasantness . . . There was stupidity maybe but no unpleasantness . . .

AL. Tell her I'm getting into my coat. (*He is putting coat on.*) Tell her I got one sleeve on.

WILLIE. (*Into phone.*) I was hoping it would work out too . . . I bent over backwards and forwards. He didn't bend sideways . . .

AL. I got the other sleeve on . . . Tell her I'm up to my hat and then I'm out the door.

WILLIE. It's a question of one word, darling. Enter! . . . Enter, that's all it comes down to.

AL. (*Puts his hat on.*) The hat is on. I'm bundled up, tell her.

WILLIE. (*Into phone.*) Yes . . . yes, I will . . . I'll tell him myself. I promise . . . Goodbye, Dorothy. (*He hangs up.*) I told her we'll give it one more chance.

AL. Not if you say "Enter." "Come in" I'll stay, "Enter," I go.

WILLIE. Ask me "knock knock knock."

AL. Don't fool around with me. I got enough pains in my neck. Are you going to say "Come in?"

WILLIE. Ask me "Knock knock knock!"

AL. I know you, you bastard!

WILLIE. ASK ME "KNOCK KNOCK KNOCK!"

AL. KNOCK KNOCK KNOCK!

WILLIE. (*Grinding it in.*) EN-TERRR!

AL. BEDBUG! CRAZY BEDBUG! (*Running out.*)

WILLIE. (*Big smile.*) ENN-TERRRR! (*The curtain starts down.*)

AL. (*Heading for the door.*) LUNATIC BASTARD!

WILLIE. ENNN-TERRRR!

CURTIN

THE GOOD DOCTOR

Premièred November 27, 1973
at the Eugene O'Neill Theatre, New York City

Directed by A. J. Antoon

CAST

"The Governess"
    Frances Sternhagen, Marsha Mason

"The Audition"
    Christopher Plummer, Marsha Mason,
    Rene Auberjonois

"The Arrangement"
    Christopher Plummer, Marsha Mason

The *Good Doctor* is twelve vignettes sprung from the creative imagination of a Writer/Narrator. Each, with ironic humor, is an incisive comment on social interaction and the human condition. Homage to Anton Chekhov is obvious.

"The Governess."
From Act I, Scene iii:
Julia—20-25
Mistress—30-45

Julia is a fearful, humbled employee during the time of the czars. Even though she is being "cheated" by her current mistress, she is acquiescent, afraid that speaking up will result in her losing her job. Even though her mistress is "cheating" her, she is paying her something (her last mistress didn't pay her a ruble). Her response to being asked if it is possible to be so submissive speaks volumes about the repressive society in which she lives.

The Mistress is employing dubious logic in order to deduct from her pay:

MISTRESS. But you get paid good money to watch everything . . . I explained that in our first meeting. Perhaps you weren't listening. Were you listening that day, Julia, or was your head in the clouds?

JULIA. Yes, M'am.

MISTRESS. Yes, your head was in the clouds?

JULIA. No, M'am. I was listening.

MISTRESS. Good girl. So that means another five rubles off (*Looks in book.*) . . . Ah yes . . . the sixteenth of January I gave you ten rubles.

JULIA. You didn't.

MISTRESS. But I made a note of it. Why would I make a note of it if I didn't give it to you?

JULIA. I don't know, M'am.

MISTRESS. That's not a satisfactory answer, Julia. . . Why would I make a note of giving you ten rubles if I did not in fact give it to you, eh? . . . No answer? . . . Then I must have given it to you, mustn't I?

JULIA. Yes, M'am. If you say so, M'am.

MISTRESS. Well, certainly I say so. That's the point of this little talk. To clear these matters up . . . Take 27 from 41, that leaves . . . fourteen, correct?

JULIA. Yes, M'am. (*She turns away, softy crying.*)

MISTRESS. What's this? Tears? Are you crying? . . . Has something made you unhappy, Julia? Please tell me. It pains me to see you like this. I'm so sensitive to tears . . . What is it?

JULIA. Only once since I have been here have I ever been given any money and that was by your husband. On my birthday he gave me three rubles.

MISTRESS. Really? There's no note of it in my book . . . (*Writes in book.*) Three rubles . . . Thank you for telling me . . . Sometimes I'm a little lax with my accounts . . . Always short-changing myself . . . So then, we take three more from fourteen, leaves eleven . . . Do you wish to check my figures?

JULIA. There's no need to, M'am.

MISTRESS. Then we're all settled. Here's your salary for two months, dear. Eleven rubles. (*She puts pile of coins on desk.*) Count it.

JULIA. It's not necessary, M'am.

MISTRESS. Come, come. Let's keep the records straight. Count it.

JULIA. (*Reluctantly counts it.*) One, two, three, four, five, six, seven, eight, nine, ten . . . ? There's only ten, M'am.

MISTRESS. Are you sure? Possibly you dropped one . . . Look on the floor, see if there's a coin there.

JULIA. I didn't drop any, M'am. I'm quite sure.

MISTRESS. Well, it's not there on my desk and I *know* I gave you ten rubles . . . Look on the floor.

JULIA. It's alright, M'am. Ten rubles will be fine.

MISTRESS. Well, keep the ten for now. And if we don't find it on the floor later, we'll discuss it again next month.

JULIA. Yes, M'am. Thank you, M'am. You're very kind M'am. (*She curtsies and then starts to leave.*)

MISTRESS. Julia! (Julia *stops, turns.*) Come back here. (*She crosses back to the desk and curtsies again.*) Why did you thank me?

JULIA. For the money, M'am.

MISTRESS. For the money? . . . But don't you realize what I've done? . . . I've cheated you . . . robbed you . . . I have no such notes in my book . . . I made up whatever came into my mind. Instead of the eighty rubles which I owe you, I gave you only ten. . . I have actually stolen from you and still you thank me . . . Why?

JULIA. In the other places I have worked, they didn't give me anything at all.

MISTRESS. Then they cheated you even worse than I did . . . I was playing a little joke on you. A cruel lesson just to teach you. You're much too trusting and in this world this is very dangerous . . . I'm going to give you the entire eighty rubles. (*Hands her an envelope.*) It's all ready for you. The rest is in this envelope. Here, take it.

JULIA. As you wish, M'am. (*She curtsies and starts to go again.*)

MISTRESS. Julia! (Julia *stops.*) . . . Is it possible to be so spineless? . . . Why don't you protest? Why don't you speak up? Why don't you cry out against this cruel and unjust treatment? . . . Is it really possible to be so guileless, so innocent . . . such a—pardon me for being so blunt—such a simpleton?

JULIA. (*The faintest trace of a smile on her lips.*) . . . Yes, M'am . . . it's possible. (*She curtsies again and runs off. . . The* Mistress *looks after her a moment, a look of complete bafflement on her face . . . The lights fade.*)

"The Audition."
From Act II, scene ii:
Girl—20-25
Voice (male)

An inexperienced young girl has come from Odessa to audition for Chekhov (Voice). He attempts to dissuade her due to her lack of professionalism, but she convinces him to allow her to read a speech from his play The Three Sisters. *Her rendition is surprisingly good, resulting in her being recalled by Chekhov.*

Chekhov has tried his best to reject the parvenu, but her persistence and flattery prevail:

VOICE. . . . Well, you're an honest little thing, aren't you? . . . It's refreshing . . . Irritating, but refreshing . . . Very well, what are you going to read for me?

GIRL. I should like to read from "The Three Sisters."

VOICE. Indeed? . . . Which sister?

GIRL. All of them . . . if you have the time.

VOICE. *All* of them? . . . Good heavens. Why don't you read the entire play while you're at it.

GIRL. Oh, thank you, sir . . . I know it all . . . Act One . . . (*She looks up.*) . . . "A drawing room in the Prozorov's house. It is midday, a bright sun is shining through the large French doors . . ."

VOICE. *That's not necessary!* . . . An excerpt will do nicely, thank you.

GIRL. Yes, sir . . . I would like to do the last moment of the play.

VOICE. Good. Good. That shouldn't take too long . . . Whenever you're ready.

GIRL. I've been ready for six months . . . Not counting the three months I waited to get on the six month waiting list.

VOICE. PLEASE, begin!

GIRL. Yes, sir . . . (*She clears her throat, then just about to begin.*) Oh, sir, could you please say, "Ta-ra-ra-boom-de-ay, sit on the curb I may." . . .

VOICE. Certainly not. Why would I say such an idiotic thing?

GIRL. I don't know, sir. You wrote it . . . Chebutykin says it at the end of the play . . . It would help me greatly if you could read just that one line . . . I've waited for six months, sir . . . I walked all the way from Odessa . . .

VOICE. Alright, alright. . . Very well, then . . . ready?

GIRL. Yes, sir.

VOICE. . . . "Ta-ra-ra-boom-de-ay, sit on the curb I may" . . .

GIRL. And Masha says, "Oh, listen to that music. They are leaving us. One has gone for good. Forever. We are left alone to begin our life again . . . We must live . . . we must live . . ." And Irina says, "A time will come when everyone will know what all this is for . . . (*She is reading with more feeling and compassion then we expected.*) . . . why there is all this suffering, and there will be no mysteries, but meanwhile we must love . . . we must work, only work . . . Tomorrow I shall go alone, and give my whole life to those who need it . . . Now it is autumn, soon winter will come and cover everything with snow, and I shall go on working, working . . ." . . . Shall I finish?

VOICE. (*Softly.*) Please.

GIRL. And Olga says, ". . . The music plays so gaily, so valiantly, one wants to live. Oh, My God. Time will pass, and we shall be gone forever . . . we'll be forgotten. Out faces will be forgotten, our voices, and how many there were of us, but out sufferings will turn into joy for those who live after us, happiness and peace will come on this earth, and then they will remember kindly and bless those who are living now. Oh, my dear sisters, it seems as if just a little more and we shall know why we live, why we suffer . . . If only we knew . . . If only we knew . . ." (*It is very still.*) Thank you, sir.

That's all I wanted. . . You've made me very happy . . . God bless you, sir. (*She walks off the stage . . . The stage is empty.*)
VOICE. (*Softly.*) . . . Will someone go to her before she walks all the way back to Odessa.

"The Arrangement"
From Act II, scene iv:
Father—40-50
Girl—20-25
(The Boy is a voice off.)

A father decides it is time for his son to be initiated in the ways of love. Here, on the street, in the underbelly of the city, he bargains with a prostitute:

FATHER. (*Leaving his son to approach the girl.*) No! Stand there! Don't move! . . . I'll be right back . . . and don't twiddle with your hat . . . This is not hat twiddling business. (*He crosses to Girl.*) Good evening, Madame . . . A lovely April night, wouldn't you say?
GIRL. Is it April already? . . . I don't get out very much.
FATHER. No, I can well understand that . . . It's er . . . it's been a long time since I've been involved in such matters, but I would like to discuss with you a subject of some delicacy.
GIRL. 30 Rubles!
FATHER. So much for the delicacy . . . 30 Rubles you say . . . Well, speaking for myself, I would say 30 Rubles is quite fair . . . But it's not for me. It's for my young, inexperienced son. That's him! The one with the knees buckling.
GIRL. It's still 30 Rubles, sir. We don't have children's prices down here.
FATHER. No, of course not . . . But 30 Rubles does seem a bit high for a boy of 19. . . Would you consider 15 Rubles?

GIRL. For 15 Rubles I read Peter Rabbit. Sir, a Norwegian ship is due here tonight and I have to go in and put on my blonde wig.

FATHER. Wait! . . . There is an extenuating circumstance . . . It's the boy's birthday and I wanted to give him a nice gift . . . what do you say?

GIRL. How about an umbrella?

FATHER. See here. In my day 30 years ago, I shared the pleasure of the most delightful girl on this street . . . Ilka the Milkmaid she was called, and she cost me a mere 10 Rubles.

GIRL. Well, she's still here, if you want her she's down to six Rubles now.

FATHER. Certainly not, good heavens . . .

BOY. (*Off.*) Father? Oh, Father?

FATHER. Yes?

BOY. (*Off.*) Am I ready yet?

FATHER. In a minute . . . I'm still shopping. . . (*To Girl.*) He's really a lovely boy . . . fragile and sweet . . . Tells me the most delightful stories . . . I'm sure you'll find him entertaining.

GIRL. Haven't you got it the wrong way around, sir?

BOY. (*Off.*) I'm getting chilly.

FATHER. (*To son.*) Well, run around, jump up and down. Be patient. You've waited nineteen years, it's just another few minutes . . . (*To Girl.*) 20 Rubles . . . not a Kopeck more . . . There's just so much I'm willing to spend on education. Please, it's for my boy.

GIRL. (*Looks at him, then smiles.*) Settled! . . . You're a good and loving father, sir, and I respect you for it . . . If I had a father like you I would have never ended here on the streets bargaining with fathers like you.

FATHER. (*Puzzled.*) I'm sure there's a moral in there somewhere, I just don't see it yet . . . Settled for 20 Rubles . . . (*Gives her the money.*) . . . Oh, there's just one other request I have . . . At the conclusion of the evenings festivities, I would appreciate it greatly if you would just say, "Happy Birthday from Poppa." . . .

GIRL. (*Nods.*) "Happy Birthday from Poppa." . . . Would you like any candles, sir?

FATHER. That's not necessary. Just be gentle and kind to him . . . Gentleness, that's all I ask . . . (*He wipes his eye.*) Good heavens, a tear . . . What a thing to cry over. . .

GIRL. I'll wait upstairs . . . two flights up, second door to the left . . . I'll be gentle, sir.

FATHER. Thank you. The girls nowadays seem to be so much more understanding.

GIRL. May I say, it's men like you who make me proud to serve my profession.

GOD'S FAVORITE

Premièred December 11, 1974
at the Eugene O'Neill Theatre, New York City

Directed by Michael Bennett

CAST

Joe Benjamin	Vincent Gardenia
Ben Benjamin	Lawrence John Moss
Sarah Benjamin	Laura Esterman
Rose Benjamin	Maria Karnilova
David Benjamin	Terry Kiser
Mady	Rosetta LeNoire
Morris	Nick LaTour
Sidney Lipton	Charles Nelson Reilly

The action of the play takes place in the Benjamin mansion on the North Shore of Long Island.

Joe Benjamin is a fifty-six-year-old self-made man. From meager beginnings he has, with ingenuity and industry, built a dynasty from the manufacture and sales of cardboard boxes. As a result, he now lives an opulent lifestyle with his family on their Long Island Estate. Joe is a truly good man, a religious, philanthropic man who gives fifty percent of his earnings to charity. Unfortunately, he is also plagued by the profligate behavior of his eldest son, David, a boy he loves in spite of his indiscretions.

Late one evening Joe is visited by Sidney Lipton, a three-dimensional messenger of God who works for Him out of his home in Jackson Heights. He has been chosen to deliver the message that Joe is God's favorite and that God, as a test of faith, has bet the Devil that Joe is the one man in the universe who will never renounce Him.

In spite of Lipton's warnings of the pain and problems that will be visited upon him, Joe refuses to sign a renunciation. As a result, Joe's faith is sorely tested: his factory burns to the ground, his business flounders, he is beset with physical ailments that inflict excruciating pain, his mansion is razed by fire and, in a crowning blow, David goes off on a drunken binge and Joe is abandoned by his family. But Joe is still resolute in his refusal to renounce God.

In a final test of faith, when Joe refuses to renounce God even though He has blinded David, the test ends, the family returns and profligate son David has an epiphany ending his dissolute ways.

From Act I:
Joe—55-60
Sidney Lipton—Ageless

Sidney, God's messenger, has told Joe that God has bet the Devil that Joe is the only person on earth who will never renounce Him, even under the greatest pressure, pain, and misery the Devil can inflict. Hearing this, Joe is resolute in his loyalty to God, stating he will never renounce Him.

Near the end of the act, Joe's cardboard box factory goes up in flames. The test has begun.

JOE. Renounce God? You think I would renounce God?
LIPTON. Tonight, no. When they shut off your steam, who knows?

JOE. You think so little of man that he would renounce *God* in the face of adversity?

LIPTON. I've seen people with a burning engine on a 747 who would sell out God in a second for a little good news from the pilot . . . So you believe me—good. I can deliver my message and run. (*Takes out a folded, dirty scarp of paper.*) You ready?

JOE. Let me see that.

LIPTON. (*Pulls away.*) I have to read it. It's not official unless I read it . . . (*He takes a pillow from the sofa, throws it on the floor, and indicates that* Joe *should knell on it.* Joe *looks around hesitantly.* Lipton *nods that it's all right.* Joe *reluctantly gets on his knees, feeling foolish and embarrassed.*) Here we go. "Joseph Marvin Benjamin . . ."

JOE. Melvin.

LIPTON. What?

JOE. Joseph *Melvin* Benjamin.

LIPTON. (*Squints at the paper.*) Melvin—right. Would you believe God has such a lousy handwriting? . . . Joseph Melvin Benjamin of 118 Park Place Drive, Oyster Bay, Long Island, zip 11771—"

JOE. Come on, come on, get on with it.

LIPTON. "Husband of Rose, father of David, Ben, and Sarah, son of Arnold and Jeanette—"

JOE. Get to the *message* already!

LIPTON. "To Joseph Melvin Benjamin, devoted husband and father . . . if you cherish your children and wife, the house that shelters you, the clothes that warm you and the flesh that covers you, if pain, calamity and disaster do not in any manner whatsoever appeal to you, then renounce your God!" That's it! Message delivered. No tip necessary, it's taken care of. Good night, good luck, God bless you . . . but I doubt it! (*He puts the message back in his pocket and starts for the French door.*)

JOE. Wait a minute! Where are you going?

LIPTON. If I had a choice, Fort Lauderdale . . . Unfortunately, the bus stop! (*He turns and starts out again.*)

JOE. It doesn't make sense. Why? Why should I, a man who has believed in God all his life, suddenly renounce him?

LIPTON. I take home a hundred-thirty-seven dollars a week. If you want theological advice call Billy Graham. Can I get the number fifteen bus on this corner?

JOE. I will *not* renounce God. I will *never* renounce God, do you hear me?

LIPTON. Renounce, don't renounce, what do I care? . . . I have to walk out in the freezing snow wearing Supphose.

JOE. I am a servant of God, He is my Maker. I fear Him and Love Him but come hell or high water, I will never renounce Him!

LIPTON. Can I be honest? You can count on the hell and high water. Good luck, Joe. I know you've got what it takes. And no matter what terrible things happen to you, remember that God loves you!

JOE. And I love Him!

LIPTON. But in case the romance falls apart, here's my number. Renouncements are toll-free calls.

(*We hear a fire engine clanging in the distance.*)

JOE. What's that?

LIPTON. I don't know.

JOE. What's going on out there?

LIPTON. (*Looks out window.*) Looks like a fire. Near the water . . . Where's your factory?

JOE. Near the water.

LIPTON. Ohh . . . Look at that burn. Like a cardboard box.

JOE. Cardboard boxes.

LIPTON. Ohh . . . Well, I wouldn't worry unless I got a phone call.

(*The* Phone *rings. They both look at it.*)

JOE. It's not my plant. My plant is a hundred percent fireproof. (*He picks up the phone.*) Hello? . . . Eddie? . . . What is it? . . . What?

LIPTON. One more "what" and you're in trouble.

JOE. (*Into the phone.*) WHAT?

LIPTON. What is it, a disaster or a calamity?

JOE. (*Into the phone.*) *The whole plant?*

LIPTON. Oh, a catastrophe, wonderful!

JOE. Thank you, Eddie . . . I know it wasn't your fault. (*He hangs up.*)

LIPTON. How much did the insurance cover?

JOE. (*He is dazed.*) I didn't have insurance. I didn't believe in insurance . . . GOD was my insurance.

LIPTON. Really? Well, that was your mistake. Even God is with John Hancock . . . So long, Joe. (*And he is gone.*)

CALIFORNIA SUITE
(V)

Premièred June 10, 1976
at the Eugene O'Neill Theatre, New York City

CAST
"Visitor from New York."

Hannah Warren	Tammy Grimes
William Warren	George Grizzard

CAST
"Visitor from Philadelphia"

Marvin Michaels	Jack Weston
Bunny	Leslie Easterbrook
Millie Michaels	Barbara Barrie

CAST
"Visitors from Chicago"

Mort Hollender	Jack Weston
Beth Hollender	Barbara Barrie
Stu Franklyn	George Grizzard
Gert Franklyn	Tammy Grimes

California Suite is comprised of four one-act plays whose action takes place in rooms 203 and 204 in the Beverly Hills Hotel.

"Visitor from New York."
From Act I, scene i:
Hannah and Billy—40-45

Hanna and Billy are divorced. She lives in New York City, he in Los Angeles. On the final day of her stay on The Coast, they meet to discuss shared-custody of their daughter, Jenny. The meeting is quickly reduced to cutting innuendo, sharp repartee, and verbal jousting.

BILLY. (*Gets up, starts towards door, stops.*) What do you want to do about Jenny?
HANNAH. Who?
BILLY. Do you want to discuss this problem sensibly and sincerely, or do you want to challenge me to the *New York Times* Crossword puzzle for her?
HANNAH. Oh, stop pouting. You may dress like a child, but you don't have to act like one.
BILLY. Would you mind terribly if I said, "Up yours" and left?
HANNAH. What have you done to her, Billy? She's changed. She used to come back to New York after the summers here taller and anxious to see her friends . . . Now she meditates and eats alfalfa.
BILLY. She just turned seventeen. Something was bound to happen to her.
HANNAH. You have no legal rights to her, of course you understand that.
BILLY. Certainly.
HANNAH. Then tell her to come home with me.
BILLY. I did. She would like to try it with me for a year. She's not happy in New York, Hannah.

HANNAH. Nobody's happy in New York. But they're *alive.*

BILLY. I can't fight you. If you want to take her, then take her. But I think you're making a mistake.

HANNAH. She still has another year of high school left.

BILLY. Believe it or not, they have good schools here. I can show you some, if you like.

HANNAH. Oh, that should be fun. Something like the Universal Studio tour?

BILLY. What a snob you are.

HANNAH. Thank God there's a few of us left.

BILLY. What is there so beautiful about your life that makes it so important to put down everyone else? Forty square blocks bounded by Lincoln Center on the west and Cinema II on the east is not the center of the goddamn universe. I grant you it's an exciting, vibrant, stimulating, fabulous city, but it's not Mecca . . . it just smells like it.

HANNAH. The hell with New York! Or Boston or Washington or Philadelphia. I don't care where Jenny lives, but *how.* She's an intelligent girl with a good mind. Let it grow and prosper. But what the hell is she going to learn in a community that has valet parking just to pick up four bagels and the *Hollywood Reporter?*

BILLY. I've been to Martha's Vineyard in July, Hannah. Heaven protect me from another intellectual Cape Cod summer . . . The political élite queuing up in old beach sandals to see Bogart pictures, standing there eating ice cream cones and reading the *New Republic.*

HANNAH. Neat, wasn't it?

BILLY. No. Your political friends never impressed me . . . I remember one hot Sunday afternoon in Hyannisport when our ambassador to some war-torn Middle Eastern country was in a state of despair because he couldn't get the hang of throwing a Frisbee. My God, the absurdity . . . I went to a charity luncheon in East Hampton to raise money for the California grape pickers. There was this teeming mob of women who must have spent a total of twelve thousand dollars on new Gucci pants in order to raise two thousand dollars for the grape pickers . . . Why the hell didn't they just mail them the pants?

HANNAH. You were terrific when you used to write like that . . . I didn't see the last picture you wrote, but they tell me it grossed very well in backward areas.

BILLY. Jesus, was I anything like you before?

HANNAH. I couldn't hold a candle to you.

BILLY. No wonder no one spoke to me here for the first two years.

HANNAH. Lucky you.

BILLY. Look, I don't want to interrupt your train of venom, but could we get back to Jenny?

"Visitor from Philadelphia."
From Act I, scene ii:
Marvin and Millie—40-45

After a night of drunken indiscretion, Marvin has awakened to the stark reality there is a woman in his bed. And she is in a morning-after stupor that has left her as limp as a dish rag. His panic is understandable, but nothing compared to the terror he experiences when his wife, Millie, arrives early from Philadelphia. Finally, after hysterical, clumsy efforts to keep Millie from discovering the "body" in his bed, he has no choice other than to come clean:

MARVIN. (*He gets up from floor, walks away.*) Millie, I can't keep this up anymore. I'm going to get a heart attack . . . I've got something to tell you.

MILLIE. What, Marvin? What is it, darling?

MARVIN. It was never my intention to hurt you, Millie, but it's very possible in the next few minutes you may be terribly, terribly hurt.

MILLIE. Is it major or minor?

MARVIN. To me it's minor, to you I think it's going to be extremely major.

MILLIE. Tell me, Marvin . . . It couldn't be that bad, as long as you're not trying to cover up something.

(Bunny *unconsciously pushes the covers down and reveals herself—but at that moment Millie is facing the other way.*)

MARVIN. (*Alarmed, he looks up at the ceiling because he doesn't know where else to look;* Millie *looks up also.*) There's something I'd like to show you, Millie. But I'm going to ask you to do something for me first . . . Say nothing for ten seconds. Whatever comes to mind, please, for the sake of both of us, say nothing for ten seconds . . . You may turn around now, Millie.

(*She turns her head around to the right and sees the body in the bed. She looks at it, and suddenly laughs aloud.*)

MILLIE. One . . . two . . . three . . . I'm praying, Marvin . . . I'm praying the maid came in here to clean, got dizzy from overwork and fainted in your bed . . . I pray to God the maids in this hotel wear pajamas.

MARVIN. It's not the maid, Millie . . . It's a woman.

MILLIE. Then I hope it's a doctor . . . Is this your doctor, Marvin? If it's not your doctor, then you're going to need a lawyer.

MARVIN. It's not a doctor, Millie . . . It's a woman.

MILLIE. That was my *third* guess. You can call American Airlines and tell them to forget my luggage. I won't be needing it . . . Let me ask you a silly question, Marvin. Why doesn't she move?

MARVIN. I can explain that.

MILLIE. If you tell me you have been carrying on with a helpless paralytic, I won't buy it, Marvin. DON'T PLAY ON MY SYMPATHY!

MARVIN. She had six margaritas and a bottle of vodka. She won't wake up till tomorrow . . . Millie, I deny nothing.

MILLIE. Interesting, because I accuse you of EVERYTHING! (*She sits on the chair and starts to put on her shoes.*) Is it a hooker, Marvin? Is it someone you know, or is it a hooker? If it's a hooker, I'm going to divorce you. If it's someone you know, I'm going to kill you.

MARVIN. I don't know her. I never met her. She's probably a hooker, I didn't ask.

MILLIE. The humiliation. The humiliation of lying in bed next to a sleeping hooker and telling you I've got my period.

MARVIN. Millie, will you please give me a chance to admit my guilt? I know you're going to take everything else away from me, at least leave me my guilt.

MILLIE. You tell that hooker to give you back your pajamas, because that's all I'm leaving you. (*She starts towards the phone. He blocks the way.*)

MARVIN. Is that all you care about? Retribution? What about fifteen years of marriage? Weren't they good years?

MILLIE. They were *terrific* . . . but I never bothered looking on the other side of the bed. (*She tries for the phone again.*)

MARVIN. Five minutes . . . If I can't win you back in five minutes, then I'm not worth holding on to.

MILLIE. Thank God you told me. Can you imagine if I fell asleep and woke up with *her* in my arms?

MARVIN. I have sinned. I have transgressed. I have committed adultery.

MILLIE. In her condition, it's necrophilia! . . . Get out of my way.

MARVIN. She was awake—drunk but awake. We were both drunk. Do you think I would do something like this *stone sober?*

MILLIE. Statements like that are not in the direction of winning me back . . . (*Into the phone.*) Operator, get me the bell captain, please. (*To* Marvin.) And let me tell you something else: Being cruel to the children is Number Two. *This* is Number One!

MARVIN. To *you*, Millie . . . I can understand where this is important to you. To me, it was meaningless.

MILLIE. That's a shame, Marvin. I always get so upset when you have a good time. (*Looks at the lifeless body.*) Look how she doesn't move. No wonder it wasn't too much fun. Hello, I'd like a taxi, please. Mrs. Michaels, Room 203. Thank you. (*Hangs up.*) I'll probably get the same cab she came in.

"Visitors from London."

From Act II, scene ii:
Diana and Sidney—40-45

Diana Nichols is a British star who has been nominated for best actress and has come to Los Angeles accompanied by her husband, Sidney, an antique dealer and discreet homosexual. Their relationship, while compatible, is one of convenience.

Diana has lost to another actress and they have returned to the hotel early in the AM. Diana, feeling the effects of alcohol, derides Sidney for his homosexual advances, and vents her frustration:

DIANA. The strangest thing happened when I lost, Sidney. I actually felt your body relax . . . When Miss Big Boobs ran up there, all teary-eyed and bouncing flesh, I felt all the tension release from every part of you. What could have caused such joy, I wondered to myself. Happy that it was finally over . . . or just happy?

SIDNEY. What a nasty streak you have when you drink . . . also when you eat and sit and walk.

DIANA. Oh, that's perverse, Sidney. Why are you so perverse tonight? Picky, picky, picky . . . Are you unhappy because you didn't get to wear my dress?

SIDNEY. If I had worn your dress, darling, it would have hung properly. Nothing personal

DIANA. There never *is* anything personal with us. Or is that getting too personal?

SIDNEY. Diana, I am sincerely sorry you lost tonight. But look at it this way. It's just a little bald, naked statue.

DIANA. Just like you'll be one day. (*Struggling with her zipper.*) Would you please get this chiffon tent off me. If you help me, I'll let you sleep in it tonight. (*He unzips her gown.*)

SIDNEY. We are taking a turn for the worse, Diana . . . Let's try and stay as sweet as we were.

DIANA. Tell me . . . Did he happen to carve his phone number in the butter patty for you?

SIDNEY. Oh, go to hell.

DIANA. To hell? What's this? A direct assault? A frontal attack? That's not like you, Sidney.

SIDNEY. You make me sick sometimes.

DIANA. When, Sidney? *Any*time at your convenience.

SIDNEY. When you can't have what you want, you make certain everyone around you will be equally miserable.

DIANA. I haven't noticed any *equals* around me . . . And I'm not miserable. I'm a artist. I'm certainly unhappy.

SIDNEY. It's amazing how you can throw up verbally as well as you can nutritionally. (*He hangs up his shirt in the closet.*)

DIANA. Adam—wasn't that his name? Adam, the first man . . . not very appropriate for you, is it? . . . He did look very Californian, I thought. Sort of a ballsy Doris Day.

SIDNEY. Oh, Christ, Diana, come off it. We keep up a front for everyone else, why can't we do it for ourselves?

DIANA. You mean lie to each other that we're perfectly well-mated? A closet couple—is that what we are, Sidney?

SIDNEY. I have never hidden behind doors, but I *am* discreet.

DIANA. Discreet? You did everything but lick his artichoke.

SIDNEY. Let's not have a discretion contest. I have heard about your lunch breaks on the set. The only thing you don't do in your dressing room is dress . . . I'm going to take some Librium. If I'm not up by nine, I've overdosed. (*He crosses into the bathroom. She gets her gown off.*)

DIANA. I wouldn't like that, Sidney. What would I do without you?

SIDNEY. (*From bathroom.*) Everything, darling.

DIANA. I'm serious. Don't ever say that to me again. I will not have you dying.

SIDNEY. I'll never be far from you. I've left instructions to be cremated and left in a pewter mug near your bed . . . Ash was always a good color for me.

DIANA. Why is he coming to England?

SIDNEY. Who?

DIANA. That boy. He said, "See you in London next week." What is he doing in London?

SIDNEY. Acting, of course. He's making a film there . . .

DIANA. What film?

SIDNEY. I don't follow other people's films. I barely follow yours. (*He comes out of the bathroom in his pajamas.*)

DIANA. (*Furious, throws her dress on the floor.*) Goddamn him and goddamn you! (*She kicks the dress across the room.*) Goddamn the Oscars, goddamn California, goddamn everything! (Sidney *looks at her.*)

SIDNEY. What is there about this climate that brings out the religion in you?

DIANA. You bastard, answer the question. Why don't you love me?

SIDNEY. What is *that* line from?

DIANA. You son-of-a-bitch, answer the question. Why don't you love me?

SIDNEY. It doesn't sound like a question.

DIANA. I am tired of paying for everything and getting nothing back in return.

"Visitors from Chicago."
From Act II, scene iii:
Beth and Mort—25-35

After traveling together for three weeks, the Hollenders' and Frank-lyns' tolerance for each other has grown precariously thin. And then Beth Hollender is injured in a tennis match with the Franklyns that Mort Hollender describes as a "war."

Here, moments after her injury, Beth and Mort return to their room. They are in tennis clothes, sweaty, Mort carrying tennis rackets and balls. Beth is hobbling on one foot, supported by Mort because she has obviously injured her ankle:

MORT. Easy . . . Easy, now . . .

BETH: Slowly . . . Go slowly . . . Please go slowly.

MORT. I'm going as slow as I can.

BETH. Then go slower . . . Mort, I'm slipping.

MORT. I got you.

BETH. I'm slipping, I'm telling you! Put down the tennis balls? I got a broken foot.

MORT. (*He drops the balls from his left hand, which was around her waist.*) It's not broken. If it was broken, you couldn't step down on it.

BETH. I can't step down on it. I'm telling you, it feels broken. It's my foot, isn't it? Put me down in here.

MORT. Which chair would you like?

BETH. (*Sarcastic.*) The one in my bedroom at home. You want to get it for me?

MORT. What are you getting upset for?

BETH. Because you ask me such stupid questions. The sofa, all right? (*He heads her for the nearest chair.*) Easy . . .

MORT. (*Tries to easy her into the chair.*) I'm trying.

BETH. *Put the goddamn rackets down!*

MORT. Sorry! I'm sorry. (*He drops the rackets, still holding her in a half standing-half sitting position.*)

BETH. (*She lowers herself into the chair.*) Oh, shit . . . Oh shit shit shit shit!

MORT. (*Nods sympathetically.*) It really hurts, heh?

BETH. When have you heard me say shit five times?

MORT. Let me try to get a doctor,

BETH. First get me some aspirins.

MORT. How many do you want?

BETH. Forty! (Mort *starts for the bathroom.*)

MORT. The thing that kills me is that they saw your shoelaces were untied. That's why they kept lobbing over your head.

BETH. Look at that ankle puff up. It's the size of a grapefruit. I'll have to wear you shoe on the plane tomorrow.

MORT. (*In the bathroom.*) And they just kept lobbing the ball over your head—lob lob lob, the sons-of-bitches.

BETH. When I fell, I heard something snap. I said to myself, "Please, God, let it be my brassiere."

MORT. (*Comes out with water and aspirin.*) That wasn't tennis out there, that was *war!* They only hit it to you when the sun was in your eyes, and they only hit it to me when my shorts were slipping down.

BETH. Will you get the doctor?

MORT. (*Angry and frustrated.*)Who? I don't know any doctors in Los Angles.

BETH. Look in the Yellow Pages under orthopedic.

MORT. On Sunday? July Fourth? You expect a doctor to make a house call on Sunday July Fourth?

BETH. Mort, it's getting excruciating. If you can't get a doctor, call a druggist . . . I'll take a laundry man, a delivery boy, just get *some*body, please!

MORT. (*Thumbs through the phone book with frustration.*) Lob lob lob, dirty sons-of-bitches . . . (*He stops at a page, runs his finger down it.*) All right, here's the orthopedics . . . Abel, Abernathy, Abromowitz, Barnard, Benson, Berkowitz . . . Pick one.

BETH. None of them sound good.

MORT. What do you mean, they don't *sound* good? They're just names . . . You want them to come over and audition for you?

BETH. Nothing strikes me . . . Keep reading.

MORT. Block, Brewster, Brunckhorst . . .

BETH. No, I don't want Brunckhorst.

MORT. What's wrong with Brunckhorst?

BETH. He sounds like a horse doctor. Get me somebody with a soft name.

MORT. This is crazy. I'll call the hotel. They must know a doctor. (*He picks up the phone.*)

BETH. Quick, cover the phone, here comes another obscenity!

MORT. (*Into the phone.*) Can I have the front desk, please?

BETH. Oh, *shity shit!*

CHAPTER TWO

Premièred on December 4, 1977
at the Imperial Theatre, New York City

Directed by Herbert Ross

CAST

George Schneider	Judd Hirsch
Leo Schneider	Cliff Gorman
Jennie Malone	Anita Gillette
Faye Medwick	Ann Wedgeworth

The action of the play takes place in Jennifer Malone's upper East Side apartment and George Schneider's lower Central Park West apartment.

George Schneider is a forty-two-year-old writer living a dour, monastic existence since losing Barbara, his wife of twelve years. His concerned older brother, Leo, an unhappily married womanizer, is determined to find George companionship and arranges a series of ridiculous liaisons before recommending that he meet Jennie Malone, a divorced actress he has met through their mutual friend Faye Medwick. George resists the meeting as does Jennie, who is still suffering the aftershocks of a very bad former marriage. But an accidental phone call from George results in them getting together for a quick, noncommittal, five-minute "look." The "look," however, proves to be to their mutual satisfaction, and after a whirlwind romance of two weeks, and over Leo's objections, they decide to marry.

Leo's unheeded warnings that George was not ready for marriage seems prophetic when George and Jennie return from their honeymoon in a state of acrimony. George cannot overcome the deep-seated psychological impediment of accepting happiness because doing so would mean that he would have to let go of Barbara. Rather than facing the problem, George accepts a writing assignment on The Coast as a means of running. But Jennie is committed. She loves George and won't give him up without a fight. Her strength and solidarity make George realize how much he loves and needs her, and gives him the courage to put Barbara behind him and face happiness without fear.

The subplot, which greatly strengthens the message of the main story, involves an affair between the womanizing Leo and married Faye. Here, in diametric contrast to George and Jennie, is a portrait of people floundering, attempting to find happiness without real love and commitment.

From Act I, scene vi:
Jennie—30-35
George—40-45

Due to a phone number mix-up, George inadvertently called Jennie resulting in them agreeing to meet at her apartment for a five-minute "look." Both are pleased with what they see.

GEORGE. I'll tell you the truth. You're not the first girl Leo's introduced me to. There were three others . . . All ranked with such disasters as the *Hindenburg* and Pearl Harbor,

JENNIE. *Now* I see. That's when the five-minute Plan was born,

GEORGE. Necessity is the Mother of Calamity.

JENNIE. Tell me about them.

GEORGE. Oh, they defy description.

JENNIE. Please. Defy it.

GEORGE. All right. Let's see. First there was Bambi. Her name tells you everything.

JENNIE. I got the picture.

GEORGE. Then there was Vilma. A dynamite girl.

JENNIE. Really?

GEORGE. Spent three years in a Turkish prison for carrying dynamite . . . Need I go on?

JENNIE. No, I think I've had enough.

GEORGE. Since then I've decided to take everything Leo says with a grain of panic . . . And now I feel rather foolish because I was very flippant with you on the phone, and now I find myself with an attractive, intelligent and what appears to be a very nice girl.

JENNIE. You won't get a fight from me on that.

GEORGE. With an appealing sense of adventure.

JENNIE. You think so?

GEORGE. It's your five minutes, too.

JENNIE. I was wondering why I said yes. I think it's because I really enjoyed talking to you on the phone. You're very bright, and I found I had to keep on my toes to keep up with you.

GEORGE. Oh. And is that unusual?

JENNIE. I haven't been on my heels in years . . . What kind of books do you write?

GEORGE. Ah, we're moving into heavy territory. What kind of books do I write? For a living I write spy novels. For posterity, I write good novels. I make a good living, but my posterity had a bad year.

JENNIE. Name some books.

GEORGE. From column A or column B?

JENNIE. Both.

GEORGE. Well, I write the spy novels under the name of Kenneth Blakely Hyphen Hill.

JENNIE. Hyphen Hill?

GEROGE. You don't say the hyphen, you just put it in.

JENNIE. Oh, God, yes. Of course. I've seen it. In drugstores, airports . . .

GEORGE. Unfortunately, not libraries.

JENNIE. Who picked the name?

GEORGE. My wife. You see, my publisher said spy novels sell better when they sound like they were written in England. We spent our honeymoon in London, and we stayed at the Blakely Hotel, and it was on a hill and the hall porter's name was Kenneth . . . If we had money in those days, my name might be Kenneth Savoy Grill.

JENNIE. And from column B?

GEORGE. I only had two published. They were a modest failure. The means "Bring us more but not too soon."

JENNIE. I'd like to read them someday.

GEORGE. I'll send you a couple of cartons of them.

(*They both sip their wine. He looks around, then back at her.*) I'm forty-two years old.

JENNIE. Today?

GEORGE. No. In general.

JENNIE. Oh. Is that statement of some historic importance?

GEORGE. No. I just wanted you to know, because you look to be about twenty-four and right now I feel a rather inept seventeen, and I didn't want you to think I was too young for you.

JENNIE. I'm thirty-two. (*They look at each other. It's the first time their gaze really holds.*)

GEORGE. Well. That was very nice, wasn't it? I mean, looking at each other like that.

JENNIE. I wasn't scrutinizing.

GEORGE. That's okay, I wasn't prying.

JENNIE. My hunch is that you're a very interesting man, George.

GEORGE. Well, my advice is—play your hunches.

JENNIE. Can I get you some more wine?

GEORGE. No thanks. I think I'd better be going.

JENNIE. *Oh? . . .* Okay.

(*They rise.*)

GEORGE. Not that I wouldn't like to stay.

JENNIE. Not that you're not welcome, but I understand.

GEORGE. I think we've hit it off very well, if you've noticed.

JENNIE. I've noticed.

GEORGE. Therefore, I would like to make a regular date. Seven to twelve, your basic normal hours.

JENNIE. Aha! With grown-up clothes and make-up?

GEORGE. Bath, shower—everything.

JENNIE. Sounds good. Let's make it.

GEORGE. You mean now?

JENNIE. Would you rather go home and do it on the phone?

GEORGE. No, no. Dangerous. I could get the wrong number and wind up with Mrs. Jurgens . . . Let's see, what is this?

JENNIE. Tuesday.

GEORGE. How about Wednesday?

JENNIE. Wednesday works out well.

GEORGE. You could play hard to get and make it Thursday.

JENNIE. No. Let's stick with Wednesday and I'll keep you waiting for half an hour.

GEORGE. (*At the door.*) Fair enough. This was nice. I'm very glad we met, Jennie.

JENNIE. So am I, George.

GEORGE. I can't believe you're from the same man who brought us Bambi and Vilma.. (*He goes. She closes the door, smiles and heads for her bedroom. The lights fade.*)

From Act I, scene viii:
Jennie—30-35
George—40-45

Even though George is crazy about Jennie, he is afraid of letting go of his feelings for his deceased wife. When he explains this to Jennie, she comforts him with understanding and love.

GEORGE. I can't believe it's just a week. I feel like we're into our fourth year or something.

JENNIE. Have you felt that, too? As though it's not a new relationship at all. I feel like we're picking up in the middle somewhere . . . of something that started a long, long time ago.

GEORGE. That's exactly how it was when I walked in your door that night last week. I didn't say to myself, "Oh how pretty. How interesting. I wonder what she's like." I said, "Of course. It's Jennie. I know her. I never met her but I know her. How terrific to find her again."

JENNIE. It's nice bumping into you again for the first time, George. (*They smile and kiss again. She looks up at him. He seems to have a pained expression on his face.*) What is it? . . . Is it the pain again? (*He shakes his head "no," then turns away to hide his tears. He takes out a handkerchief to wipe his eyes.*) George! Oh, George, sweetheart, what? Tell me. (*She cradles his head in her arms as he tries to fight back his emotions.*)

GEORGE. I don't know, Jennie.

JENNIE. It's all right . . . Whatever you're feeling, it's all right.

GEORGE. I keep trying to push Barbara out of my mind . . . I can't do it. I've tried, Jennie.

JENNIE. I know.

GEORGE. I really don't want to. I'm so afraid of losing her forever.

JENNIE. I understand and it's all right.

GEORGE. I know I'll never stop loving Barbara, but I feel so good about you . . . and I can't get the two things together in my mind.

JENNIE. It all happened so fast, George. You expect so much of yourself so soon.

GEORGE. On the way over in the cab tonight, I'm yelling at the cab driver, "Can't you get there faster?" . . . And then some nights I wake up saying, "I'm never going to see Barbara again and I hope to God it's just a dream."

JENNIE. I love you, George . . . I want you to know that.

GEORGE. Give me a little time, Jennie. Stay next to me. Be with me. Just give me the time to tell you how happy you make me feel.

JENNIE. I'm not going anywhere, George. You can't lose me. I know a good thing when I see it.

GEORGE. (*Managing a smile.*) Jeez! I thought I had food poisoning and its just a mild case of ecstasy.

JENNIE. (*Embraces him.*) I just want you to be happy. I want you to have room for all your feelings. I'll share whatever you want to share with me. I'm very strong, George. I can work a sixteen-hours day on a baloney sandwich and a milk shake. I have enough for both of us. Use it, George. Please. Use me . . .

GEORGE. (*Wipes his eyes, puts the hanky down.*) Really? Would you knit me a camel's-hair overcoat?

JENNIE. With or without humps? (*Touches his hand.*) Why did it scare you so, George? We were sitting there touching hands, and you suddenly broke into a cold sweat.

GEORGE. Because its not supposed to happen twice in your life.

From Act II, scene v:
Jennie—30-35
George—40-45

George and Jennie have just returned to his apartment from their honeymoon. But it is far from a joyous occasion because George is still fixated on his deceased wife, Barbara.

GEORGE. (*A deep breath.*) Jesus, I don't have the strength for this kind of thing anymore.
JENNIE. You were doing fine two minutes ago.
GEORGE. (*Looks at his hands.*) Sweating like crazy . . . I'm sorry, Jennie. I don't think I'm up to this tonight.
JENNIE. Why, George? Why is it so painful? What are you feeling now? Do you think that I'm expecting you to behave a certain way?
GEORGE. No. *I* expect it. I expect a full commitment from myself . . . I did it twelve years ago . . . But I can't do it now.
JENNIE. I'm in no hurry. What you're giving now is enough for me. I know the rest will come.
GEORGE. *How* do you know? How the hell did you become so wise and smart? Stop being so goddamn understanding, will you? It bores the crap out of me.
JENNIE. Then what *do* you want? Bitterness? Anger? Fury? You want me to stand toe to toe with you like Barbara did? Well, I'm not Barbara. And I'll be damned if I'm going to recreate *her* life, just to make *my* life work with you. This is our life now, George, and the sooner we start accepting that, the sooner we can get on with this marriage.
GEORGE. No, you're not Barbara. That's clear enough.

JENNIE. (*Devastated.*) Oh, Jesus, George. If you want to hurt me, you don't have to work that hard.

GEORGE. Sorry, but you give me so much room to be cruel, I don't know when to stop.

JENNIE. I never realized that was a *fault* until now.

GEORGE. I guess It's one of the minor little adjustments you have to make. But I have no worry—you'll make them

JENNIE. And you resent me for that?

GEORGE. I resent you for *everything!*

JENNIE. (*Perplexed.*) *Why, George, Why?*

GEORGE. Because I don't feel like making you happy tonight! I don't feel like having a wonderful time. I don't think I *wanted* a "terrifically wonderful" honeymoon! You want happiness, Jennie, find yourself another football player, will ya? I resent everything you want out of marriage that I've already had. And for making me reach so deep inside to give it to you again. I resent being at L or M and having to go back to A! And most of all, I resent not being able to say in front of you . . . that I miss Barbara so much. (*He covers his eyes, crying silently.* Jennie *has been cut so deeply, she can hardly react. She just sits there, fighting back her tears.*) Oh, Christ, Jennie, I'm sorry . . . I think I need a little outside assistance.

JENNIE. (*Nods.*) What do you want to do?

GEORGE. (*Shrugs.*) I don't know . . . I don't want to make any promises I can't keep.

JENNIE. Whatever you want.

GEORGE. We got, as they say in the trade, problems, kid. (*He goes to her, embraces her head, then goes into the bedroom, leaving her stunned and alone.*)

I OUGHT to BE in PICTURES

Premièred April 3, 1980
at the Eugene O'Neill Theatre, New York City

Directed by Herbert Ross

CAST

Libby	Dinah Manoff
Steffy	Joyce Van Patten
Herb	Ron Liebman

The action of the play takes place in a small bungalow in West Hollywood, California.

Herb Tucker is a down-on-his-luck scriptwriter living in a run-down rental in West Hollywood. He hasn't been productive for some time and rationalizes that the state of the industry is the reason he isn't connecting. In truth, he has become an unmotivated procrastinator with a defeatist attitude. Herb's longtime, sleep-over girlfriend is Steffy Blondell, an attractive forty-year-old who is a make-up artist at Columbia Pictures. She is Herb's anchor and friend and attempts, to no avail, to motivate him and boost his confidence.

When Herb's nineteen-year-old daughter, Libby, arrives unexpectedly from New York, they are unable to relate; he hasn't seen her for sixteen years since he walked out on his wife, Libby, and his son, Robby. Libby tells Herb that she has come to the Coast to get into pictures, but in truth she is there because she is bereft of love and desperately needs to make a familial connection. But it is difficult for Herb to give of himself and make commitments, an aspect of his personality that has also become a problem for Steffy, who wants more than the occasional night in his bed.

Libby, a self-sufficient girl, moves into the bungalow and transforms it from a depressing environment to one that is bright and cheerful. She can apparently do anything. She even tunes up Herb's old Mustang. Then she wrangles a job as a valet, parking cars for Hollywood's rich and famous. When Herb takes her to task for her pipe dream of being a movie star, she retaliates, rightfully accusing him of being a negative procrastinator. The ensuing conflict climaxes with Libby spilling her real feelings—she wants to be unconditionally loved. This results in a touching scene during which father and daughter open the floodgates of true emotion.

Libby, haven gotten the emotional support she came for, announces that she is returning to New York. Then in a crowning maneuver, during a phone call home, she prods Herb into speaking with her mother and his son, Robby. Then she departs as she came—unceremoniously, leaving in her wake an enlightened Herb.

From Act I, scene I:
Steffy—35-40
Herb—40-45

When Herb's daughter, Libby, walks off after a heated confrontation, his sometime live-in girlfriend, Steffy, takes him to task for his lack of parental understanding and dilatory work-ethic.

STEFFY. Let her stay a couple of days. It's none of my business, Herb, but you owe her that much. She's probably still on the corner waiting for the bus.

HERB. You were right before. It's none of your business.

STEFFY. (*She's stopped cold.*) Sorry.

HERB. Steffy, why do you bother with me? I'm hardly ever nice to you. I make love to you all night and don't say two civil words to you in the morning. You're still an attractive woman. (*Peeks at clock.*) It's only nine-twenty. If you get an early start, I bet you could find someone out there who would really appreciate you.

STEFFY. I thought I'd give you ten more minutes.

HERB. If you can say that after two years, you're a very patient lady.

STEFFY. Yeah. Either that or stupid.

HERB. I see other women, you know.

STEFFY. I know. But you didn't have to tell me.

HERB. Well, I *am* faithful in a way. I don't tell them about *you*.

STEFFY. I don't see other men, if you're interested.

HERB. I appreciate that.

STEFFY. It's not that I don't look. I'm just not crazy about what's out there.

HERB. I know. I'm really special, right?

STEFFY. I never really ask myself what the attraction is. The truth might scare the hell out of me.

HERB. Well, I know why you turn *me* on.

STEFFY. I do too. Because I'm not looking for a husband.

HERB. Noooo . . . Well, that's part of it. You turn me on because you never make any demands. You never push me. I wonder what you would say if I really asked you to marry me.

STEFFY. I don't know. Ask me.

HERB. (*Laughs.*) Foxy. I love foxy ladies. (*He kisses her cheek.*) You should be a writer.

STEFFY. (*Pointedly.*) So should you. (*He turns away.*) I mean it. You make me so damn furious sometimes. You're got more talent than ninety percent of the hacks in this town and you're too lazy or too scared to put it down on paper. Why don't you?

HERB. Because the other ten percent have all the jobs.

STEFFY. You know what you need? You need to have someone shove a ten-foot Roman candle up your rear end and set it off.

HERB. So how come every time I ask you to do kinky stuff in bed, you always get sore at me?

STEFFY. I'm going to work. (*She picks up her purse.*)

HERB. Come on, give me a little smile?

STEFFY. It's impossible to have a serious discussion with you.

HERB. I'm being very serious. I would love to kiss you all over, including your pocketbook.

STEFFY. I think I'm going to take the picture in Hawaii. Three months out of the country may do us a lot of good.

HERB. Are you kidding? You couldn't go three months without me. It's not possible.

STEFFY. Damn it, Herb. I don't like you today.

HERB. Go on, you're crazy about me.

STEFFY. I know that, but I still don't like you today. (*Starts for the door.*) Don't call me until you get five pages written. I don't care if it's lousy, I don't care if you copy it out of George Bernard Shaw, as long as it's five pages. And don't bother phoning me because I won't take your calls.

From Act II, scene iv:
Libby—20
Herb—40-45

When Libby returns home at 3 A.M. from parking cars at a Beverly Hills party, she is confronted by Herb who scolds her for not informing him of her late-night peregrinations. After a brief confrontation, the conversation turns serious, leading to a touching scene between father and daughter during which Libby expresses her deep-seated feelings of abandonment and desperate need of uncon-ditional love.

When Libby asks Herb pointed questions about his early sexual relationship with her mother, he is reluctant to deal with the subject.

LIBBY. No, you didn't. I knew she lied. She just couldn't talk to me about those things. That's why I'm talking to you. I wanted to know how she felt. If she was scared or excited. Was it fun? Was it painful? I don't think it was an unreasonable question. I mean, she could teach me how to walk, why couldn't she teach me how to love?
HERB. I don't know.
LIBBY. So what was she like? Making love.
HERB. Libby, there's just so much I can handle.
LIBBY. Because she was so angry when you left, you took her with you. That's why I was so angry with you. It was bad enough you were gone, but you could have left my mother there for me.
HERB. She *was* there for you. Look, if she didn't want to see other men, that was *her* choice. Maybe *you* were the other men in her life.
LIBBY. Yeah. No wonder I grew up to be a fruitcake.
HERB. Don't talk like that.
LIBBY. She used to hug me so hard sometimes. Like she was trying to squeeze all the love out of me that she wasn't getting anywhere else. So instead of growing up to be me, I grew up to be a substitute—
HERB. You're no substitute. You're first-string all the way. I never saw a girl your age who was so sure of herself. Jesus, if I had *half* your confidence, maybe you'd have been parking *my* car at that party tonight.
LIBBY. Confidence? . . . I'm scared from the minute I wake up in the morning.
HERB. Of what?

LIBBY. Of everything. I get up an hour before you just to check if you're still there . . . I know Grandma's dead. I know she probably can't hear me. But I speak to her everyday anyway because I'm not so sure anyone else is listening. If I have to go for an interview, my heart pounds so much you can see it through my blouse. That thing about writing my name on the valet stubs? It wasn't my idea. It was Gordon's. He did it first, so I just copied him . . . If you want the God's honest truth, I don't even want to be an actress. I don't know the first thing about acting. I don't know *what* I want to be . . . (*Beginning to break down.*) I just wanted to come out here and see you. I just wanted to know what you were like. I wanted to know why I was so frightened every time a boy wanted to reach out and touch me . . . I just wanted somebody in the family to hold me because it was *me,* Libby, and not somebody who wasn't there . . .

(*She is sobbing. He quickly reaches out and grabs her in his arms.*)

HERB. I'm here, baby, I'm here. It's all right. Don't cry. I'm holding you, baby, I'm holding you.

(*He cradles her in his arms as she sobs silently.*)

FOOLS

Premièred on April 6, 1981
at the Eugene O'Neill Theatre, New York City

Directed by Mike Nichols

CAST

Leon Tolchinsky	John Rubinstein
Snetsky	Gerald Hiken
Magistrate	Fred Stuthman
Slovitch	David Lipman
Mishkin	Joseph Leon
Yenchna	Florence Stanley
Dr. Zubritsky	Harold Gould
Lenya Zubritsky	Mary Louise Wilson
Sophia Zubritsky	Pamela Reed
Gregor Yousekevitch	Richard B. Shull

The action of the play takes place in the town of Kulyenchikov in the year 1890.

Leon Tolchinsky is ecstatic. He has landed a terrific job as a schoolteacher in the idyllic Russian hamlet of Kulyenchikov. But when he arrives, he finds people sweeping dust from the stoops *back into* their homes, and people who think that if you milk a cow upside down, you get more cream. Kulyenchikov, it seems, has been cursed with chronic stupidity for two hundred years, and the desperate townspeople have hired Leon, hoping he can break the curse. But they don't tell him that if he stays more than twenty-four hours—and fails to break the curse—he also becomes stupid. Why doesn't Leon leave, you say? Because he has fallen in love with the beautiful daughter of the town doctor. She is so stupid she that has only recently learned how to sit down. Of course, Leon breaks the curse and gets the girl.

From Act I, scene i:
Leon—25-30
Snetsky—30-50

Upon his arrival in Kulyenchikov, when Leon is greeted by the shepherd, Snetsky, he suspects, even though outwardly the town appears to be charming, that things aren't what the seem.

(Snetsky *carries a ram's horn and a staff.*)

LEON. I am Leon Steponovitch Tolchinsky and I am to be the new schoolteacher.
SNETSKY. Is that a fact? (*He shakes Leon's hand vigorously.*) I'm very honored to meet you, Leon Steponovitch Tolchinsky. I am Something Something Snetsky . . . Will you be staying the night?
LEON. You don't understand. Kulyenchikov will be my new home. I'm going to live here and teach here. I am, if I may say so, an excellent teacher.
SNETSKY. Oh, they all were. They came by the thousands, but not one of them lasted through the first night. (*He blows the horn hard.*) Oh, it's so hard to blow these, I don't know how the sheep do it.
LEON. You've had thousands of teachers?

SNETSKY. More. Hundreds! We're unteachable. We're all stupid. There isn't a town more stupid in all of Mother Poland.

LEON. Russia.

SNETSKY. Whatever. All good people, mind you, but not a decent brain among them. (*He blows the horn with difficulty.*) Oh, that feels so good. I just opened up my ears. I thought you were whispering. What were you saying?

LEON. Are you telling me that every man, woman and child—

SNETSKY. All stupid. Including me. Talk to me another ten minutes and you'll begin to notice.

LEON. (*Ignores it.*) I was hired by Dr. Zubritsky to teach his young daughter.

SNETSKY. (*Bursts out laughing.*) Teach his daughter? Impossible. The girl is hopeless. Nineteen years old and she just recently learned to sit down . . . She's hopeless. She doesn't even know the difference between a cow and a duck. Not that it's an easy subject, mind you.

LEON. (*To the audience.*) Something is up here! (*He takes the ad out of his pocket.*) I thought nothing of it then, but when I first read it I *did* notice that every word in the advertisement was misspelled . . . I'm sure Dr. Zubritsky will explain it all to me. (*He steps back and turns to* Snetsky.) You're been most helpful, Citizen Snetsky. I enjoyed our chat.

SNETSKY. As did I, Master Tolchinsky. (*He turns to the audience.*) He's not the only one who can have private thoughts. I can have private thoughts as well. (*He tries to think.*) The trouble is, I can never think of a thought to have in private. Oh, I must be on my way. Good day, schoolmaster.

From Act I, scene i:
Leon—25-30
Sophia—20-25

If Leon does not educate the lovely Sophia within one hour, the curse of stupidity will not be broken and he, too, will become its victim. But the task ahead is daunting—she has only recently learned to sit and has trouble remembering her own name.

SOPHIA. Am I finished with one plus one?

LEON. You are if you remember the answer.

SOPHIA. I remembered it before. Is it necessary to remember it again?

LEON. Of course it's necessary to remember it again. It's necessary to remember it for *always.*

SOPHIA. You mean you will always be asking me what one plus one is?

LEON. No! Once you tell me, we can move on to other things. Like one plus two and one plus three, and so on. But if you can't remember what one plus one is, then the answer to one plus two is meaningless.

SOPHIA. Do you know how much one plus one is?

LEON. Certainly.

SOPHIA. Then why is it necessary for me to know? Certainly, if you have so much esteem and affection for me, you will tell me the answer whenever I ask you.

LEON. But I won't always be around to tell you. You have to know yourself. In case other people ask you.

SOPHIA. No one here ever asks questions like that. Even if I told them, they wouldn't know if it was the right answer.

LEON. Because they are cursed with ignorance. And we are trying to lift that debilitating affliction.

SOPHIA. You're getting angry with me. What's the point of being educated if you get angry? When you didn't ask me such questions, you always said the loveliest things to me. Is this what it's like to be intelligent?

LEON. No, Sophia. It is I who am not being intelligent. It's frustration and impatience that drives me to such crude behavior. Forgive me. We'll start from the beginning again. One plus one is two. Repeat.

SOPHIA. One plus one is two. Repeat

LEON. *No!* Don't repeat the word "repeat." Just repeat the part before I say "repeat." . . . Now watch me carefully: One plus one is two. *Repeat!*

SOPHIA. What were you like as a little boy?

LEON. (*Angrily.*) What was I like as a little boy?

SOPHIA. You're shouting again.

LEON. (*Tries to placate her.*) I was inquisitive. Probing. Wondering why we were put on this earth and what the purpose of man's existence was.

SOIPHIA. The purpose of man's existence . . . !

LEON. (*Shouts.*) *I've heard enough of that.* Sophia, you must stop asking me questions. Our time is nearly gone.

SOPHIA. Then how am I to learn?

LEON. Sophia, you must answer what I ask, not what you want me to answer.

SOPHIA. Then I will learn only what *you* want me to know. Why can't I learn what I want to know?

LEON. Because what you want to know is of no practical value. What I want to teach is acceptable knowledge.

SOPHIA. Is knowing what you were like as a little boy not acceptable knowledge?

LEON. Of course not. It's of no significance at all.

SOPHIA. But it's much more interesting than that which is significant.

LEON. But I'm not trying to interest you. I'm trying to educate you.

SOPHIA. I know. But while you fail to educate me, you never fail to interest me. I find that very significant.

LEON. There is nothing like the logic of an illogical mind! Let's try one more time.

BRIGHTON BEACH MEMOIRS
(V L)

Premièred December 2, 1982
at the Alvin Theatre, New York City

Directed by Gene Saks

CAST

Eugene	Matthew Broderick
Blanche	Joyce Van Patten
Kate	Elizabeth Franz
Laurie	Mandy Ingber
Nora	Jodi Thelen
Stanley	Zeljko Ivanek
Jack	Peter Michael Goetz

The action of the play takes place in a home in Brighton Beach, Brooklyn, New York.

Through the narrative of Eugene Jerome, a fifteen-year-old aspiring writer, we learn of family events taking place in his Brighton Beach home in September 1937. Other than Eugene, the household is inhabited by his mother and father, Kate and Jack Jerome, his older brother, Stan, and his aunt, Blanche, and her two daughters, Kate and Nora, who have been living with the Jeromes since the untimely death of Blanche's husband. Kate Jerome is a no-nonsense workhorse who runs the household with business-like efficiently. Husband Jack is a beleaguered but benevolent provider who works two jobs in order to eke out enough money to support the brood. Stan is a good son with a strong sense of independence and who is worshipped by Eugene, who views him as worldly-wise. Blanche, Kate's younger sister, is a pretty but frail asthmatic who lives in a state of suspended self-pity and is catered to by ever-resilient Kate. Blanche's older daughter, Nora, is an attractive, stage-struck sixteen-year-old who feels constricted and unloved. And her younger daughter, Laurie, is a pampered, sickly child whose major illness is probably hypochondria.

Conflicts ignite this volatile mix when Blanche refuses to allow Nora to appear in a Broadway musical, Stanley is threatened with losing his much-needed job, and Blanche agrees to have dinner with a neighborhood alcoholic. Then, further exacerbating matters, Jack loses his part-time job and suffers a mild heart attack.

Eugene humorously chronicles and comments upon the events that are afflicting his Brighton Beach boyhood: Nora is not speaking to Blanche for refusing to allow her to participate in show business. She also misses her father, and she resents Blanche for her preferential treatment of the "sickly" Laurie. Jack is recuperating from his heart problem and needs rest and attention at a time when finances are desperately low. Kate is disturbed that, over her objections, Blanche is planning to date a man of dubious character, and when Stan loses his critical paycheck in a poker game and leaves home as a result, she emotionally unravels in an outburst, during which she accuses Blanche of being an ungrateful malingerer.

Even though the argument between Blanche and Kate is a bitter one, it ultimately has positive, cathartic effects. Blanche is awakened, and in a confrontation with Nora she exhibits new-found insight and strength. With the air now cleared, Blanche and Kate reconcile on a level of mutual understanding. And Stanley returns, unable to walk out on his family during time of crisis.

The end of the play finds the family preparing to accept Jack's cousin and his family, refugees from war-torn Poland, into their crowded quarters. Humanity abounds in Eugene's humble Brighton Beach home.

From Act I:
Nora—16
Laurie—13

Nora's enthusiasm for appearing in a Broadway musical is not shared by her mother, Blanche, who rightly feels that Nora is too young and naïve, and that getting a proper education takes prece-dence over show business. But she has not given her decision. Rather, due to the fact her brother-in-law, Jack, is the head of the household, she has deferred to him. Nora's fate is in Jack's hands.

Nora, beside herself with frustration, resents having her destiny in the hands of her uncle. Here, in a scene with her younger sister, Laurie, she expresses her lingering sense of loss for her father and her commitment to the realization of a better life.

(Nora *is crying.* Laurie *sits on the twin bed opposite her, watching.*)

LAURIE. So? . . . What are you going to do?
NORA. I don't know. Leave me alone. Don't just sit there watching me.
LAURIE. It's my room as much as yours. I don't have to leave it if I don't want to.
NORA. Do you have to stare at me? Can't I have any privacy?
LAURIE. I'm staring into space. I can't help it if your body inter-feres. (*There is a pause.*) I bet you're worried?

NORA. How would you feel if your entire life depended on what your Uncle Jack decided? . . . Oh, God, I wish Daddy were alive.

LAURIE. He would have said, "No." He was really *strict*.

NORA. Not with me. I mean he was strict but he was fair. If he said, "No," he always gave me a good reason. He always talked things out . . . I wish I could call him somewhere now and ask him what to do. One three minute call to heaven is all I ask.

LAURIE. Ask Mom. She talks to him every night.

NORA. Who told you that?

LAURIE. She did. Every night before she goes to bed. She puts his picture on her pillow and talks to him. Then she pulls the blanket half way up the picture and goes to sleep.

NORA. She does not.

LAURIE. She does too. Last year when I had the big fever, I slept in bed with both of them. In the middle of the night, my face fell on his picture and cut my nose.

NORA. She never told me that . . . That's weird.

LAURIE. I can't remember him much anymore. I use to remember him real good but now he disappears a little bit every day.

NORA. Oh, God, he was so handsome. Always dressed so dapper, his shoes always shined. I always thought he should have been a movie star . . . like Gary Cooper . . . only very short. Mostly I remember his pockets.

LAURIE. His pockets?

NORA. When I was six or seven he always brought me home a little surprise. Like a Hershey or a top. He'd tell me to go get it in his coat pocket. So I'd run to the closet and put my hand in and it felt as big as a tent. I wanted to crawl in there and go to sleep. And there were all these terrific things in there, like Juicy Fruit gum or Spearmint Life Savers and bits of cellophane and crumbled pieces of tobacco and movie stubs and nickels and pennies and rubber bands and paper clips and his grey suede gloves that he wore in the wintertime.

LAURIE. With the stitched lines down the fingers. I remember.

NORA. Then I found his coat in Mom's closet and I put my hand in the pocket. And everything was gone. It was emptied and dry cleaned and it felt cold . . . And that's when I knew he was really dead. (*Thinks a moment.*) Oh God, I wish we had our own place to live. I hate being a boarder. Listen, let's make a pact . . . The first one who makes enough money promises not to spend any on herself, but saves it all to get a house for you and me and Mom. That means every penny we get from now on, we save for the house . . . We can't buy *anything*. No lipstick or magazines or nail polish or bubble bum. *Nothing* . . . Is it a pact?

LAURIE. (*Thinks.*) . . . What about movies?

NORA. Movies too.

LAURIE. Starting when?

NORA. Starting today. Starting right now.

LAURIE. . . . Can we start Sunday? I wanted to see *The Thin Man.*

NORA. Who's in it?

LAURIE. William Powell and Myrna Loy.

NORA. Okay. Starting Sunday . . . I'll go with you Saturday.

(*They shake hands, sealing their "pact."*)

From Act I:
Kate and Jack—40

Jack, tired and beleaguered, tells Kate that the party favor company for which he worked has gone out of business.

(*Kate crosses to the front door and goes out. Jack is sitting on the stoop, wiping his neck.*)

KATE. What's wrong. Eugene said you were holding your chest.

JACK. I wasn't holding my chest.

KATE. You have to carry that box everyday? Back and forth from the city. You don't work hard enough, Jack?

JACK. You want the box, it's yours. Keep it. I don't need it anymore.

KATE. What do you mean?

JACK. Del Mars Party Favors went out of business. They closed him out. The man is bankrupt.

KATE. Oh, My God!

JACK. He never warned me it was coming.

KATE. You told me he lived up on Riverside Drive. With a view of the river. A three hundred dollar a month apartment he had. A man like that.

JACK. Who are the ones you think go bankrupt? You live in a cold water flat on Delancey Street, bankruptcy is one thing God spares you.

KATE. Alright . . . You can always find good in something. You don't have to lug that box anymore. You don't have to get up a five-thirty in the morning. We can all eat dinner at a decent hour. You still have your job with Jacobson, we won't starve.

JACK. I can't make ends meet with what I make at Jacobson's. Not with seven people to feed.

KATE. (*Looks back towards the house.*) They'll hear you. We'll talk later.

JACK. I can't get by without that extra twenty-five dollars a week. I can't pay rent and insurance and food and clothing for seven people. Christmas and New Years alone I made a hundred and fifty dollars.

KATE. (*Nervous about anyone hearing.*) Stop it, Jack. You'll only get yourself sick.

JACK. He didn't even pay me for the week, the bastard. Five salesmen are laid off and he's going to a Broadway show tonight. I stuffed every hat and noise maker I could carry in that box and walked out of there. At his funeral I'll put on a pointy hat and blow a horn. The bastard!

KATE. Don't talk like that. Something'll come up. You'll go to temple this weekend. You'll pray all day Saturday.

JACK. (*Smiles ironically.*) There's men in that temple who've been praying for forty years. You know how many prayers have to get answered before my turn comes up?

KATE. (*She rubs his back where it pains him.*) Your turn'll come up. God has time for everybody.

From Act I:
Kate—40
Blanche—38

In an effort to get sister Blanche socially involved, she invites her to accompany her and Jack to Jack's annual business affair. But Blanche has other plans—a prior engagement. When Kate discovers these plans include a certain Mr. Murphy, a man she finds detestable from both a societal and ethnic standpoint, she expresses her displeasure in no uncertain terms.

BLANCHE. I've made plans for next Wednesday night.

KATE. More important than this? They have this affair one a year.

BLANCHE. I'm having dinner with someone.

KATE. You're having dinner? With a man? That's wonderful. Why didn't you tell me?

BLANCHE. With Mr. Murphy. (*This stops* Kate *right in her tracks.*)

KATE. Who's Mr. Murphy? . . . Oh, My God! I don't understand you. You're going to dinner with that man? Do you know where he'll take you? To a saloon. To a Bar and Grill, that's where he'll take you.

BLANCHE. We're going to Chardov's, the Hungarian Restaurant. You never met the man, why do you dislike him so much?

KATE. I don't have to meet that kind. I just have to smell his breath when he opens the window. What do you think a man like that is looking for? I grew up with that kind on Avenue A. How many times have Stanley and Gene come home from school black and blue from the beatings they took from those Irish hooligans? What have you got to talk to with a man like that?

BLANCHE. Is that why you don't like him? Because he's Irish? When have the Jews and the Irish ever fought a war? You know who George Bernard Shaw is?

KATE. I don't care who he is.

BLANCHE. One of the greatest Irish writers in the world? What would you say if *he* took me to Chardov's next Wednesday?

KATE. Is Mr. Murphy a writer? Tell him to bring me some of his books. I'll be glad to read them.

BLANCHE. Kate, When are you going to give up being an older sister?

KATE. I've heard stories about him. With women. They like their women, you know. Well, if that's what you want, it's your business.

From Act I:
Stan—18-19
Jack—40

Stan has acted on principle and stood up for a wrongly-accused black man at work, even going so far as to sweep dirt on his employer's shoes. The result is, he will be terminated unless he writes a letter of apology to his employer. Torn between principles and reality, he has confronted his father with the dilemma:

JACK. Oh, Stanley, Stanley, Stanley!

STAN. I'm sorry, Pop.

JACK. You shouldn't have swept dirt on his shoes.

STAN. I know.

JACK. Especially in front of other people.

STAN. I know.

JACK. He's your boss. He pays your salary. His money helps put food on our dining table.

STAN. I know, Pop.

JACK. And we don't have money to waste. Believe me when I tell you that.

STAN. I believe you, Pop.

JACK. You were sick three days last year and he only docked you a day and a half's pay, remember that?

STAN. I know, I can see what you're getting at. I'll write the letter. I'll do it tonight.

JACK. On the other hand, you did a courageous thing. You defended a fellow worker. Nobody else stood up for him, did they?

STAN. I was the only one.

JACK. That's something to be proud of. It was what you believed in. That's standing on your principles.

STAN. That's why I didn't want to write the letter.

JACK. The question is, can this family afford principles right now?

STAN. It would make it hard, I know.

JACK. Not just on you and me. But on your mother. On Aunt Blanche, Nora, Laurie.

STAN. Eugene.

JACK. Eugene would have to get a part-time job. Time he should be using studying books to get himself somewhere.

STAN. He wants to be a writer. He wants to go to college.

JACK. I wish I could have sent *you*. I've always been sick about that, Stanley.

STAN. I like working, Pop. I really do . . . Listen, I made up my mind. I'm going to write the letter.

JACK. And how will your principles feel in the morning?

STAN. My principles feel better already. You told me you were proud of what I did. That's all I really cared about.

JACK. You know something, Stanley. I don't think there's much in college they could teach you that you don't already know.

STAN. Guess who I learned it from? . . . Thanks for talking to me, Pop. See you in the morning . . . You coming to bed?

STAN. I think I'll sit here for a while. It's the only time of day I have a few minutes for myself.

From Act II:
Eugene—15
Stan—18-19

Jack—driving a taxi part-time as a means of generating income—has suffered a mild heart attack and is home recuperating and, as a consequence, Stan's salary is the family's only means of support. But Stanley has been profligate, losing his entire paycheck in a poker game. When Stan tells Eugene he also once squandered money on a prostitute and Eugene asks typically juvenile questions, Stan vents his frustrations on his younger brother.

EUGENE. What happened to the five dollars? Do you gamble that too?

STAN. No. I gave it to a girl . . . You know. A pro.

EUGENE. A pro what? . . . A PROSTITUTE? You went to one of those places? Holy shit!

STAN. I'm not going to warn you about that word again.

EUGENE. Is that what it costs? Five dollars?

STAN. Two fifty. I went to this guy I know. He still owes me.

EUGENE. And you never told me? What was she like? Was she pretty? How old was she?

STAN. Don't start in with me, Eugene.

EUGENE. Did she get completely naked or what?

STAN. (*Furious.*) Every time I get in trouble, I have to tell you what a naked girl looks like? . . . Do me a favor, Eugene. Go in the bathroom, whack off and grow up by yourself.

EUGENE. Don't get sore. If you were me, you'd ask the same questions.

STAN. Well, I never had an older brother to teach me those things. I had to do it all on my own. You don't know how lucky you are to be the younger one. You don't have the responsibilities I do. You're still in school looking up girls' dresses on the staircase.

EUGENE. I work plenty hard in school.

STAN. Yeah? Well, let me see your report card. Today's the first of the month, I know you got it. I want to see your report card.

EUGENE. I don't have to show you my report card. You're not my father.

STAN. Yes, I am. As long as Pop is sick, I am. I'm the only in the family who's working, ain't I?

EUGENE. Really? Well, where's your salary this week, Pop?

STAN. (*Grabs* Eugene *in anger.*) I hate you sometimes. You're nothing but a lousy shit. I help you all the time and you never help me without wanting something for it. I hate your disgusting guts.

EUGENE. (*Screaming.*) Not as much as I hate yours. You snore at night. You pick your toe nails. You smell up the bathroom. When I go in there I have to puke.

STAN. (*Screaming back.*) Give me your report card. Give it to me, God dammit, or I'll bash your face in.

EUGENE. (*Starts to cry.*) You want it? Here! (*He grabs it out of a book.*) Here's my lousy report card . . . you fuck! (*He falls on the bed crying, his face to the wall. Stanley sits on his own bed and reads the report card. There is a long silence.*)

STAN. (*Softly.*) . . . Four As and a B . . . That's good. That's real good, Eugene . . . You're smart . . . I want you to go to college . . . I want you to be somebody important someday . . . Because I'm no . . . I'm no damn good . . . I'm sorry I said those things to you.

EUGENE. (*Still faces the wall. It's to hard to look at Stanley.*) . . . Me too . . . I'm sorry too.

From Act II:
Nora—16
Blanche—38

Nora is still smarting over Blanche's decision not to allow her to participate in a Broadway production. She is disrespectful, bitchy, and judgmental. When Blanche angrily tells her that Nora has no right to judge her, Nora lashes out, exploding in an outburst of deep-seated feelings. Blanche responds to Nora's outburst, showing grit and determination, committing herself to a future without self-recrimination and self-pity.

NORA. *Judge* you? I can't even talk to you. I don't exist to you. I have tried so hard to get close to you but there was never any room. Whatever you had to give went to Daddy, and when he died, whatever was left you gave to—(*She turns away.*)

BLANCHE. What? Finish what you were going to say.

NORA. . . . I have been jealous my whole life of Laurie because she was lucky enough to be born sick. I could never turn a light on in my room at night or read in bed because Laurie always needed her precious sleep. I could never have a friend over on the weekends because Laurie was always resting. I used to pray I'd get some terrible disease or get hit by a car so I'd have a leg all twisted or crippled and then once, maybe just once, *I'd* get to crawl in bed next to you on a cold rainy night and talk to you and hold you until I fell asleep in your arms . . . just once . . . (*She is in tears.*)

BLANCHE. My God, Nora . . . Is that what you think of me?

NORA. It isn't any worse than what you think of me?

BLANCHE. (*Hesitates, trying to recover.*) . . . I'm not going to let you hurt me, Nora. I'm not going to let you tell me that I don't love you or that I haven't tried to give you as much as I gave Laurie . . . God knows I'm not perfect because enough angry people in this house told me so tonight . . . But I am *not* going to be a doormat for all the frustrations and unhappiness that you or Aunt Kate or anyone else wants to lay at my feet . . . I did *not* create this universe. I do *not* decide who lives and dies, or who's rich or poor or who feels loved and who feels deprived. If you feel cheated that Laurie gets more than you, then I feel cheated that I had a husband who died at thirty-six. And if you keep on feeling that way, you'll end up like me . . . with something much worse than loneliness or helplessness and that's self-pity. Believe me, there is no leg that's twisted or bent that is more crippling than a human being who thrives on his own misfortunes . . . I am sorry, Nora, that you feel unloved and I will do everything I can to change it except apologize for it. I am tired of apologizing. After a while it becomes your life's work and it doesn't bring any money into the house . . . If it's taken your pain and Aunt Kate's anger to get me to start living again, then God will give me strength to make it up to you, but I will *not* go back to being that frightened, helpless woman that I created! . . . I've already buried someone I love. Now it's time to bury someone I hate.

BILOXI BLUES

(V L)

Premièred March 28, 1985
at the Neil Simon Theatre, New York City

CAST

Roy Selridge	Brian Tarantina
Joseph Wykowski	Matt Mulhern
Don Carney	Alan Ruck
Eugene Morris Jerome	Matthew Broderick
Arnold Epstein	Barry Miller
Sgt. Merwin J. Toomey	Bill Sadler
James Hennesey	Goeffrey Sharp
Rowena	Randall Edwards
Daisy Hannigan	Penelope Ann Miller

All set pieces are representational, stylized, and free-flowing. It is 1943.

The plot of the play is propelled by the narrative of Eugene Morris Jerome, a young draftee and aspiring writer from Brighton Beach, New York who wants to achieve three things while in the service: lose his virginity, fall in love, and become a writer. Eugene and his buddies, a motley group, have been in the Army just four days before arriving for basic training at Biloxi, Mississippi where they are greeted by Sergeant Merwin J. Toomey a profane, battle-hardened disciplinarian. Toomey sadistically upbraids the boys and takes an instant dislike to Arnold Epstein, an intelligent, sensitive fellow who is as strong-willed in his beliefs as Toomey is in his. This sets up a battle of attrition between the two, during which Epstein is subjected to interminable latrine duty, racial slurs, and humiliating derision from Toomey as well as his buddies. But Epstein maintains his dignity in a wonderful example of strength of character.

While on a twenty-four-hour pass Eugene attains one of his goals—he loses his virginity to a prostitute. Back at the base, things heat up when one of the platoon is arrested for committing a homosexual act. He is identified and is carted off for punishment by Sergeant Toomey.

On the eve of his going to the veterans hospital, a drunken Toomey confronts Epstein with a loaded .45 and forces Epstein to arrest him for the crime of threatening an enlisted man while intoxicated. This is a ploy to trick Epstein into becoming an obedient, disciplined soldier. Epstein reluctantly obeys, sentencing Toomey to a hundred push-ups. The next day Toomey leaves, never to return.

Before shipping out, Eugene visits Daisy Hannigan, a nice Catholic girl he had met at the U.S.O. They express their love for each other and seal their feelings with a kiss. Eugene has accomplished his second goal—he has fallen in love.

Overseas, Eugene's buddies are disbursed to the battlefields of Europe (their fate is described in the curtain monologue at the end of this section). But Eugene is injured in a Jeep accident in England and never sees active duty. Instead he is given an assignment as a writer for *Stars and Stripes*, resulting in him achieving his final goal—he has become a writer.

Toomey—40-45
Arnold—18-20

After Sergeant Toomey has deliberately stolen sixty-two dollars from Wykowski's wallet as a means of enforcing his ideas of discipline, he is unmasked by Arnold Epstein who saw him remove the money. Toomey, who has taken a strong dislike for the intellectual Epstein, threatens heavy retribution.

TOOMEY. . . . How the hell do you think you can beat me?

ARNOLD. I'm not trying to beat you, Sergeant. I'm trying to work with you.

TOOMEY. (*Looks at him sideways.*) I think you're low on batteries, Epstein. I think some plumber turned off your fountain of knowledge. What the hell do you mean, working with me?

ARNOLD. I don't think it's necessary to dehumanize a man to get him to perform. You can get better results raising our spirits than lowering our dignity.

TOOMEY. Why in the hell did you put back money you know you didn't take?

ARNOLD. Because I knew that you did. I saw you take it. I think inventing a crime that didn't exist to enforce your theories of discipline is Neanderthal in its conception.

TOOMEY. (*Gets closer.*) I can arrange it, Epstein, that from now on you get nothing to eat in the mess hall except cotton balls. You ever eat cotton balls, Epstein? You can chew it till 1986, it don't swallow . . . Men do not face the enemy machine guns because they have been treated with kindness. They face them because they have a bayonet up their ass. I don't want them human. I want them obedient.

ARNOLD. Egyptian Kings made their slaves obedient. Eventually they lost their slaves and their kingdom.

TOOMEY. Yeah, well, I may lose mine but before you go, you're going to build me the biggest God damn pyramid you ever saw . . . I'm trying to save these boy's lives, you crawling bookworm. Stand in my way and I'll pulverize you into chicken droppings.
ARNOLD. It should be an interesting contest, Sergeant.
TOOMEY. After I crush your testicles, you can replace them with the cotton balls. (*He glares at* Arnold, *then exits quickly.*) . . . Neanderthal in its conception. Jesus Christ!

From Act II:
Eugene—18-20
Rowena—25-35

Eugene, a virgin, has decided it's time to alter this condition and visits a local prostitute with his buddies.

(Rowena's room, Eugene hidden behind a screen, Rowena sitting at her vanity, trying to be patient.)

ROWENA. (*Calls out.*) How you doing, honey?
EUGENE. (*Behind screen.*) Okay.
ROWENA. You having trouble in there?
EUGENE. No. No trouble.
ROWENA. What the hell you doing for ten minutes? C'mon, Kid. I haven't got all day. (Eugene *appears. He is wearing his khaki shorts, shoes and socks. A cigarette dangles from his lips.* Rowena *looks at him.*) Listen. You can keep your shorts on if you want but I have a rule against wearing army shoes in bed.
EUGENE. (*Looks down.*) Oh. I'm sorry. I just forgot to take them off. (*He sits on the bed and very slowly starts to unlace them. To audience:*) I started to sweat like crazy. I prayed my Aqua Velva was

working. (Rowena *sprays around her with perfume from an atomizer.*)

ROWENA. You don't mind a little perfume, do you, honey? The boy before you had on a gallon of Aqua Velva.

EUGENE. (*Looks at audience then at her.*) No, I don't mind. You can spray some on me. (*She smiles and sprays him playfully.*) Gee, it smells good.

ROWENA. If you'd like bottle for your girl friend, I sell them. Five dollars apiece.

EUGENE. You sell perfume too?

ROWENA. I sell hard to get items. Silk stockings. Black panties . . . You interested?

EUGENE. (*Earnestly.*) Do you sell men's clothing?

ROWENA. (*Laughs.*) That's cute. You're cute, honey . . . You want me to take your shoes off?

EUGENE. I can do it. Honest. I can do it. (*He gets his first shoe off.*)

ROWENA. Is this your first time?

EUGENE. My first time? (*He laughs.*) Are you kidding? That's funny . . . Noo . . . It's my second time . . . The first time they were closed.

ROWENA. You don't smoke cigarettes either, do you? (*She takes cigarette out of* Eugene's *mouth.*)

EUGENE. How'd you know?

ROWENA. You looked like your face was on fire . . . If you want to look older, why don't you try a mustache?

EUGENE. I did but it wouldn't grow in on the left side . . . What's you name?

ROWENA. Rowena . . . What's yours?

EUGENE. My name? (*To audience.*) I suddenly panicked. Supposing the girl kept a diary.

ROWENA. Well?

EUGENE. (*Quickly.*) Jack . . . Er . . . Jack Mulgroovey.

ROWENA. Yeah? I knew a Tom Mulgreevy once.

EUGENE. No. Mine is Mulgroovey. Oo not ee.

ROWENA. Where you from, Jack?

EUGENE. (*Slight accent.*) Texarkana.

ROWENA. Is that right?

EUGENE. Yes, ma'am.

ROWENA. Is that Texas or Arkansas?

EUGENE. Arkansas, I think.

ROWENA. You think?

EUGENE. I left there when I was two. Then we moved to Georgia.

ROWENA. Really? You a cracker?

EUGENE. What's a cracker?

ROWENA. Someone from Georgia.

EUGENE. Oh, yeah. I'm a cracker. The whole family's crackers . . .
Were you born in Biloxi?

ROWENA. No. Gulfport. I still live there with my husband.

EUGENE. Your husband? . . . You're married? My God! If he finds
me here he'll kill me.

ROWENA. No he won't.

EUGENE. Does he know that you're a—you're a—

ROWENA. Sure he does. That's how we met. He's in the navy. He
was one of my best customers. He still is.

EUGENE. You mean you charge your own husband?

ROWENA. I mean he's my best lover . . . You gonna do it from
there, cowboy? 'Cause I'll have to make some adjustments.

EUGENE. I'm ready. (*To Rowena.*) Here I come. (*She holds open
blanket. He gets into the bed and clings to the side.*)

ROWENA. If you're gonna hang on the edge like that, we're gonna
be on the floor in two minutes.

EUGENE. I didn't want to crowd you.

ROWENA. Crowding is what this is all about, Tex. (*She pulls him
over. He kneels above her.*) Okay, honey. Do your stuff.

EUGENE. What stuff is that?

ROWENA. Whatever you like to do.

EUGENE. Why don't you start and I'll catch up.

ROWENA. Didn't anyone ever tell you what to do?

EUGENE. My brother once showed me but you look at lot different than my brother.

ROWENA. You're sweet. I went to high school with a boy like you. I had the biggest damn crush on him.

EUGENE. (*Still above her.*) Do you have a hanky?

ROWENA. Anything wrong?

EUGENE. My nose is running. (*She takes hanky, wipes his nose.*)

ROWENA. Better?

EUGENE. Thank you. Listen, please don't be offended but I really don't care if this is a wonderful experience or not. I just want to get it over with.

ROWENA. Whatever you say . . . Lights on or off?

EUGENE. Actually I'd like a blindfold. (*She reaches over and turns off lamp.*) . . . Oh, God . . . Oh, MY GOD! (*Slumps down.*) . . . WOW! . . . I DID IT! . . . IT DID IT!

ROWENA. Anything else, honey?

EUGENE. (*Calmer, more mature.*) Yes. I'd like two bottles of perfume and a pair of black panties.

From Act II:
Toomey—45-50
Arnold—18-20

It is the night before Toomey's last day as an active member of the U.S. Army. The next morning he will be transferred to a veterans hospital for the purpose of having a steel plate in his head replaced. He is wild, piss drunk, and determined—as a final act of desperation— to turn Epstein into a real soldier.

The gun-wielding sergeant forces Arnold to arrest him for threatening the life of an enlisted man.

TOOMEY. (*Holds up gun again.*) Don't give me none of your God damn compassion, Epstein . . . Compassion is just going to get you a Star of David at the Arlington Cemetery.

ARNOLD. Yes, Sergeant.

TOOMEY. They can put 65 pounds of nuts and bolts in my head, give me a brown tweed suit and a job pumping gas, I will still be the best damn sergeant you'll ever meet in your short but sweet life, Epsteen-or-Epstine.

ARNOLD. I'm sure of that, Sergeant.

TOOMEY. One night from my room here, I heard a game being played in the barracks. I heard Jerome ask every man what they would want if they had one last week to live . . . I played the game right along with you and put my five bucks down on my bunk just like the rest of you. (*Takes out a bill.*) Here's my money. You tell me if I would have won the game.

ARNOLD. The game is over, Sergeant.

TOOMEY. Not yet, boy. Not yet . . . alright. You know what I would do with my last week on earth?

ARNOLD. What's that, Sergeant?

TOOMEY. I would like to take one army rookie, the greatest misfit dumb-ass malcontent sub-human useless son of a bitch I ever came across and turn him into an obedient, disciplined soldier that this army could be proud of. That would be my victory. You are that sub-human misfit, Epstein, and by God, before I leave here, I'm gonna do it and pick up my five dollars, you hear me?

ARNOLD. None of us actually did it, Sergeant. It was just a game.

TOOMEY. Not to me, soldier. On you feet, Epstein!

ARNOLD. Really, Sergeant, I don't think you're in any condition to—

TOOMEY. ON YOUR FEET! (Arnold *stands.*) ATTEN-SHUN! (*He snaps to attention.*) . . . A crime has been committed in this room tonight, Epstein. A breach of army regulations. A non-commissioned officer has threatened the life of an enlisted man, brandishing a loaded weapon at him without cause or provocation, the said act being provoked by an inebriated platoon leader while on duty . . . I am that platoon leader, Epstein, and it is your unquestioned duty to report this incident to the proper authorities.

ARNOLD. Look, that's really not necessary, Sergean—

TOOMEY. As I am piss drunk and dangerous, Epstein, it is also your duty to relieve me of my loaded weapon.

ARNOLD. I never really thought you were going to shoot me, Ser—

TOOMEY. TAKE MY WEAPON, GOD DAMN IT!

ARNOLD. What do you mean, take it? How am I going to take it?

TOOMEY. Demand it, you weasel bastard, or I'll blow your puny brains out.

ARNOLD. (*Calming down.*) Okay, okay . . . may I have your pistol, Sergeant?

TOOMEY. Force it out of my hand.

ARNOLD. Force it out of your hand?

TOOMEY. Grab my wrist! If you dare! (Arnold *leaps for* Toomey's *wrist, wrestling for the .45.* Toomey *finally allows him to wrest it from him.*) Good!

ARNOLD. Okay. Thanks. Now why don't we just try to get a good night's sleep and—

TOOMEY. To properly charge me, you'll need witnesses . . . Call in the platoon.

ARNOLD. The platoon? You don't want to do that in front of all—

TOOMEY. CALL THEM IN SOLDIER!

From Act II:
Eugene and Daisy—18-20

Eugene has fallen in love with Daisy, a girl he met a the U. S. O. She is demure, intelligent and seriously Catholic. Shortly before shipping out, Eugene travels from Biloxi to Gulfport see her. It is a short encounter because it is Good Friday and Daisy, strictly observant, limits their meeting to ten minutes. In this scene they express their love for each other—a new and exhilarating experience for them both.

(*Daisy is carrying a small, wrapped package.*)

DAISY. I think you're a special person, Eugene. If you want me to, I'll write you as often as you want.

EUGENE. Of course I do. I want you to write me every day. And I want a picture. I don't even have a picture of you.

DAISY. What kind of picture?

EUGENE. Do you have one where I could feel your skin?

DAISY. If I did, I wish I had one where I could squeeze your hand.

EUGENE. . . . I'm going to shoot my foot, I swear. I don't want to leave here.

DAISY. I'm glad you feel the same way about me, Eugene.

EUGENE. You know I do . . . I'd have come tonight even if I knew I had only five minutes with you . . . Daisy, I—I—

DAISY. What, Eugene?

EUGENE. I want to say something but I'm having a lot of trouble with the words.

DAISY. That doesn't sound like Eugene the Writer to me.

EUGENE. Well, I'm not writing now. I'm Eugene the talker . . . Daisy, I just want to tell you I— I— God damn it, why can't I say it? . . . Oooh! I'm sorry. I apologize. I didn't mean to say that. Especially on Good Friday.

DAISY. I'll say ten Hail Mary's for you.

EUGENE. You don't have to do that. They're not going to do me any good.

DAISY. What is it you wanted to say?

EUGENE. Ah, Daisy, you know what it is. I've never said it to a girl in my life. I don't know what it's going to sound like when it comes out.

DAISY. Say it and I'll tell you.

EUGENE. (*Takes a deep breath.*) . . . I love you, Daisy. (*He exhales.*) Ah, nuts. It came out wrong. It's not the way I meant it.

DAISY. I never heard it said so beautifully.

EUGENE. What do you mean? How many other guys have said it to you?

DAISY. None. I meant in the movies. Not Tyrone Power or Robert Taylor or even Clark Gable.

EUGENE. Yeah, well they get paid for saying it. I'm in business for myself.

DAISY. (*Laughs.*) I remember everything you say to me. When I go home at nights, I write them all down and I read them over whenever I miss you.

EUGENE. Well, if you're writing your memoirs, keep your locker closed. I don't want to be the talk of St. Mary's

(*We hear church bells chime.*)

DAISY. It's eight o'clock. I've got to go.

EUGENE. You didn't say it to me yet.

DAISY. That I love you.

EUGENE. No. Not like that. You threw it in too quickly . . . You have to take a breath, prepare for it and then say it.

DAISY. Alright. (*She inhales.*) I've taken a breath . . . (*She waits.*) Now I'm preparing for it . . . And now I'll say it . . . I love you, Eugene. (*He moves to kiss her.*) We can't kiss. It's Good Friday.

EUGENE. You have to kiss after you say "I love you." Not even God would forgive you that.

DAISY. Alright . . . I love you, Eugene. (*Kisses him lightly on the lips.*) I have to go.

EUGENE. Daisy! This is the most important moment in our lives. It's the first time we're in love. That only happens once . . . When I leave tonight, I don't know if we'll ever see each other again.

DAISY. Don't say that, Eugene. Please don't say that.

EUGENE. It's possible. I pray it doesn't happen, but it's possible . . . I need a proper kiss, Daisy. A kiss to commemorate a night I'll never forget as long as I live. (*She looks at him.*) I'll even say a hundred Hail Mary's for you on the bus ride back . . . Okay? (*She smiles and nods. He takes her in his arms and kisses her warmly and passionately . . . When they part, she seems weak.*)

DAISY. I think you'd better say two hundred on the bus . . . Oh, I almost forgot. This is for you. It's a book.

EUGENE. Really? What book? I love your taste in books.

DAISY. It's blank pages. For your memoirs. Page one can start tonight. (*She Hugs Eugene.*) Take care of yourself, Eugene Morris Jerome . . . Even if some other girl gets you, I'll always know I was your first love. (*Runs off.*)

EUGENE. I knew at that moment I was a long way from becoming a writer because there were no words I could find to describe the happiness I felt in those ten minutes with Daisy Hannigan.

BROADWAY BOUND

Premièred December 4, 1986
at the Broadhurst Theatre, New York City

Directed by Gene Saks

CAST

Kate	Linda Lavin
Ben	John Randolph
Eugene	Jonathan Silverman
Stan	Jason Alexander
Blanche	Phyllis Newman
Jack	Philip Sterling

The action of the play takes place in a house in Brighton Beach, Brooklyn, New York.

The Jeromes' Brighton Beach home is inhabited by Kate and Jack, their sons Eugene and Stan, and Kate's father, Ben. Kate is a practical homemaker, Jack is a cutter in the garment district, Eugene and Stan are aspiring comedy writers, and Ben is a cranky old Socialist who refuses to live with his wife in his granddaughter Blanche's Park Avenue apartment.

While Kate is plain and lives humbly, Blanche is pretty and wealthy and carries guilt feelings as a consequence. And her pleas with Ben to reconcile with his wife and move to Florida result in her being hurt by his cold irascibility and lack of affection.

The thirty-three-year-old marriage between Kate and Jack is strained because Kate is harboring the fact that she knows Jack had been intimate with another woman. But she has said nothing, hoping that the affair would prove transitory. But when she discovers that Jack has renewed the relationship, she can no longer remain silent and confronts him with the facts. Jack reluctantly admits to the affair. But his confession is self-satisfying. Kate is hurt and left with feelings of inadequacy and anger. Their domestic relationship degenerates into one of either referring to each other in the third person or not speaking. In the meantime, Eugene and Stan have gotten an assignment writing for a new comedy show on CBS radio. They are elated, but their elation is short-lived when Jack interprets their humor as a direct reflection upon family and friends and, more specifically, upon his act of infidelity. The boys try to reason with Jack, but his guilt renders him irrational, and when he attempts to defend his mistress, Stan stands up for his mother in a noble but relationship-fracturing outburst.

Jack moves out of the house, and when Eugene and Stan score as writers for Phil Silvers, they decide to move to New York City. They have outgrown Brighton Beach and it is time to move on. Jack eventually remarries, Ben finally succumbs to the sunny beaches of Miami, and Kate remains in her home, basking in the glory of her sons' success.

From Act I:
Stan—28
Eugene—23

Stan, a dedicated plugger, has persuaded CBS to look at a sketch written by him and his brother, Eugene. This will require all-night skulling because the network wants to see the sketch the next day. Whereas Stan is committed to working all night and foregoing dinner for a sandwich in his room, Eugene gives more weight to a date than the task at hand.

EUGENE. I didn't realize we were going to work tonight.

STAN. Well, we are . . . Put some lettuce on my sandwich.

EUGENE. The thing is, I wanted to see this girl tonight.

STAN. Well, now you won't see her. And get me some cucumbers.

EUGENE. I could leave by seven and be back by nine.

STAN. You can see her another night. What's wrong with you?

EUGENE. She's engaged to a guy from Harvard. She wants to break it off, but he's coming in tomorrow to talk her back into it. If I don't convince her I'm the guy for her, he's liable to talk her into going through with it.

STAN. If he can talk her into it, what do you want her for?

EUGENE. Because she's perfect. And you only get one chance in you life of meeting a perfect girl.

STAN. You know how many perfect girls there are in Hollywood? They're all perfect. You'll be begging for a plain one. (Eugene *goes to his own room and begins to dress for his date.* Stan *is in pursuit.*)

EUGENE. An hour and a half, that's all I'll be gone. If I don't talk to her face to face, I'll lose her, Stan. I know it.

STAN. Eugene, as much confidence as I have in us, I don't have that much confidence that we can write the sketch tonight. But we have to try. Remember the story Pop told us? How he had the opportunity to go into his own business with a friend . . . how he stayed up all night thinking about it . . . and he couldn't make up his mind. A week later it was too late. His friend lives on Park Avenue now, and Pop is still cutting raincoats . . . Maybe this is the only chance we'll ever get. Maybe not. But are you willing to risk everything for a girl you might not even be interested in next week?

EUGENE. I'll be interested in her for the rest of my life.

STAN. Then go out with her. Take as much time as you want. I'll write the sketch myself. (*Storming back to his own room.*) I Mean it. I'm not going to blow this opportunity.

EUGENE. Never mind. I won't see her.

STAN. I said, I'll do it myself.

EUGENE. (*Going downstairs.*) Don't do me any favors.

From Act I:
Kate —50
Jack—50-55

After thirty-three years, the marriage of Kate and Jack Jerome has become sub-Platonic. Jack is listless, uncommunicative, and no longer affectionate. Kate, suspecting infidelity, has confronted Jack with this. After an embarrassing interlude of denial, Jack finally opens up regarding his feelings, admits to having had an affair, tells Kate it is behind him. But Kate knows differently—she has been informed that Jack has resumed seeing the woman.

JACK. . . . So? What do you want to do?

KATE. What do *I* want to do? Is that how it works? You have an affair, and I get the choice of forgetting about it or living alone for the rest of my life? . . . It's so simple for you, isn't it? I am so angry. I am so hurt by your selfishness. You break what was good between us and leave me to pick up the pieces . . . and you *still* continue to lie to me.

JACK. I told you everything.

KATE. (*Sitting in the Upstage dining chair.*) I knew about that woman a year ago. I got a phone call from a friend. I won't even tell you who . . . "What's going on with you and Jack?" she asks me. "Are you two still together? Who's this woman he's having lunch with every day?" she asks me . . . I said, "Did you see them to-

gether?" . . . She said, "No, but I heard." . . . I said, "Don't believe
what you hear. Believe what you see!" and I hung up on her . . . Did
I do good, Jack? Did I defend my husband like a good wife? . . . A
year I lived with that, hoping to God it wasn't true and if it was,
praying it would go away . . . And God was good to me. No more
phone calls, no more stories about Jack and his lunch partner . . . No
more wondering why you were coming home late from work even
when it wasn't busy season . . . Until this morning. Guess who calls
me? . . . Guess who Jack was having lunch with in the same restaurant twice last week? . . . Last year's lies don't hold up this year, Jack
. . . This year you have to deal with it. (*Jack looks at her, remains
silent for a moment.*)
JACK. . . . It's true, I saw her last week. Twice in the same restaurant, once in another restaurant.
KATE. And where else, Jack? Do you always sit or do you lie down
once in a while? (*Rising.*) Twice tonight I went to the phone to see if
you were really working, but I was so afraid to hear that you left
early, I couldn't dial the number . . . How is it possible I could hate
you so much after loving you all my life?
JACK. Would you believe me if I told you it was lunch and nothing
more?
KATE. (*Crossing to the stairs.*) I can't talk about this anymore . . .
Sleep down here. Anywhere you want except next to me.
JACK. She's just a friend now, Kate. That's all.
KATE. Is that what you tell her I am? Just a wife? (*She starts up the
stairs.*)
JACK. She left her job for six months. I knew what had happened
but I couldn't get in touch with her. Her son was killed in an auto-
mobile accident . . . So I have lunch with her and talk about anything
else except the accident.

KATE. (*Coming back down to the foot of the stairs.*) If you see her again, you take your things and move out of the house. (*She starts back up the stairs.*)

JACK. I slept with her before and you forgave me. Now I buy the woman lunch and offer compassion and for this you want to end the marriage.

KATE. (*Coming back downstairs, close to* Jack.) I don't expect to get through a lifetime without you touching another woman. But having feelings for her is something I can never forgive.

From Act II:
Stan—28
Jack—50-55
Eugene—23

A month has passed, and the tension between Kate and Jack is evident. They are not speaking and are addressing each other in the third person. But their sons, Eugene and Stan, are elated because they have landed a job writing for a new show on CBS radio.

After the show airs, Jack is upset because he draws parallels between what the boys have written and the neighborhood and his household, and, out of underlying guilt, is particularly sensitive about dialogue that he feels called attention to his affair. The boys deny pernicious intent, but Jack is relentless, triggering a hostile exchange between him and Stan. And when Jack attempts to defend the reputation of the woman with whom he is having an affair, Stan is courageous in defense of his mother.

JACK. I will never forgive either one of you for ridiculing me in front of my neighbors, in front of my friends, in front of strangers. You'll never know how many people I called to tell to turn on the program because I was so proud of my two sons. That's a mistake I won't make again.

STAN. You may have been proud of *them,* but you never encouraged *us.* If it were up to you, I'd still be selling boys' clothing.

JACK. After what I heard tonight, I wish to God you were.

EUGENE. Stan, stop it! Cut it out! . . . I'm sorry you feel this way, Pop. We both are. But I swear, we never thought of you and Mom when we wrote the sketch. We just thought of older couples who lived in this neighborhood, but when we got it down on paper, I guess it sounded like the ones we knew best . . . It wasn't intentional, I swear. (Stan *sits in the armchair.* Jack *sits between the two boys, but talks to* Stan.)

JACK. You know what I thought when I heard it? I swear to God. I thought it was their way of getting back at me for hurting their mother . . . Is that so impossible to imagine?

STAN. No. Not so impossible.

JACK. Ah, maybe we're getting closer to the truth now . . . What did she tell you about this woman? Did she tell you what she was like?

STAN. I told you. She never talked to me about any of it.

JACK. But you seem to have feelings about it. Where did you get them from? Someone you know from New York? You have lots of friends there, right? Because let me tell you something . . . No matter what you heard about this woman, you will never find a kinder or more decent human being on the face of the earth. You understand me?

STAN. Go to hell.

JACK. What did you say to me?

STAN. I said, "Go to hell!"

EUGENE. Stan. Please. Don't do this.

STAN. (*Standing.*) I don't care if she's Joan of Arc, that's still my mother we're talking about. Do whatever you God damn please, but don't blame Gene and me of humiliating you when you're the one who's been humiliating *us* . . . You're so damn guilty for what you've done, you're accusing everyone else of betraying *you* . . . I never wanted to hear what was happening to you and Mom. I prayed every night you would both work it out and it would pass out of our lives. You could have called each other "him" and "her" forever as long as it kept you together . . . All my life you taught me about things like dignity and principles and I believed them. I still do, I guess . . . But what kind of principles does a man have when he tells his sons the woman's he's seeing on the side is a wonderful, decent human being?

JACK. (*Stands, composes himself, then walks slowly to* Stan.) Either you've grown up fast . . . Or I've outlived my place in this house. (Jack *looks at both the boys, then goes to the stairs to his bedroom and closes the door.*)

From Act II:
Kate—50
Eugene—23

Eugene loves his mother and her stories and insists she repeat the one about the time she danced with George Raft.

   At the conclusion of her story, Eugene and Kate dance together in a touching moment between mother and son.

EUGENE. Did you have a—you know—a crush on him?

KATE. On George Raft? You think I'm crazy? He was Italian. I was in enough trouble already. He wasn't my type anyway . . . Your father was the one I had the crush on . . . Since I was thirteen years old. He was five years older then me. He went with a whole other crowd. In those days young people didn't tell each other they had crushes on them. You had to guess. So you sent messages with your eyes, your face, the way you walked by them.

EUGENE. How did you walk by him?

KATE. Not too much, not too little. But he was hard to figure out. He was never a show-off, never a fancy Dan. He didn't smile a lot, but when he did, you knew he meant it. Most boys then smiled at everything. They thought it gave them a good personality. Jack was too honest to put on a good personality. He was what he was . . . and to get a smile from Jack Jerome, you knew you had to earn it . . . But it cost him plenty. The smilers got to be the salesmen. The smilers got to be the bosses. The smilers got all the girls. Your father paid the price for not being a phony . . . It was hard to impress him. That's why I went to the Primrose that night. I thought if Jack heard that I danced with George Raft, maybe I'd get him to notice me.

EUGENE. This is a movie. There's a whole movie in this story, Ma. And one day I'm going to write it.

KATE. So that night, in a pouring rain, me and Adele Abrams went to the Primrose. My hair got soaking wet, I lost my curls, I wanted to die. But then I got this brilliant idea. Instead of drying it, I combed it straight down and left it wet. Jet black hair. I looked like a Latin from Manhattan . . . The perfect partner for George Raft . . . When I walked out of the ladies' room, my own friends didn't recognize me.

EUGENE. I can't believe this is *my mother* you're talking about.

KATE. Don't worry. I knew God was going to punish me for the wet hair, too . . . Ten boys must have asked me to dance. But I said no to all of them because I didn't want to tire myself out . . . And then I started to get scared. Because it was ten after eleven and he still didn't show up. If I wasn't home by twelve, my parents would walk in and find out I was lying to them. And with my mother, I didn't need God to punish me.

EUGENE. Twelve o'clock! Cinderella! This story has everything.

KATE. And then, at twenty after eleven, he walks in . . . Like the King of Spain. My heart was beating louder than the drummer in the band . . . He had two friends with him, one on each side, like bodyguards. And I swear, there was something in their inside pockets. I thought to myself, they're either guns or more jars of grease for his hair.

EUGENE. (*To audience.*) She actually had a sense of humor. This was a side of my mother I hardly ever saw. (*To Kate.*) So, he walks in with these two guys.

KATE. (*Taking off her sweater and standing C.*) So, he walks in with these two friends and I know I don't have much time. So I grabbed Bobby Zugetti, a shoe clerk, who was the best dancer at the Primrose, and said, "Bobby, dance with me!" . . . I knew he had a crush on me and I never gave him a tumble before. He didn't know what hit him. So out on the floor we go, and we fox-trotted from one side of the ballroom and back. In and out, bobbing and weaving through the crowd, gliding across the floor like a pair of ice skaters.

EUGENE. "Begin the Beguine" . . . Maybe "Night and Day." That's what I would use in the picture.

KATE. And I never once looked over to see if George Raft was looking at me . . . I wanted to get *his* attention, I didn't want to give him mine . . . The music finishes and Bobby dips me down to the floor. It was a little lower than a nice girl should dip, but I figured one more sin wouldn't kill me . . . And I walk over to Adele, I'm dripping with perspiration, and I said, "Well? Did he watch me?" . . . And she said, "It's hard to tell. His eyes don't move." So I look over and he's sitting at a table with his two friends and Adele is right. His eyes don't move. And it's twenty-five to twelve, and he's never even noticed me. And I said to myself, "Well, if it's not meant to be, it's not meant to be." . . . And Adele and I started for the door.

EUGENE. The tension mounts. The audience is on the edge of their seats.

KATE. As we pass their table, George Raft stands up and says, "Excuse me." And he's looking right at Adele Abrams. He says, "Could

I ask you a question, please?" Adele is shaking like a leaf. And she walks over to him.

EUGENE. Adele? He's talking to Adele Abrams?

KATE. And he says, "I wonder if your friend would care to dance with me?" . . . And she says, "You want *me* to ask her?" . . . And he says, "Please. I'm a little shy."

EUGENE. I don't believe it. I don't believe George Raft said that.

KATE. I swear to God. May I never live to see another day.

EUGENE. Even if it's true, it's out of the picture. An audience would never believe it.

KATE. Fine. So Adele says, "I'll ask her." . . . So she comes back and asks me . . . And I look at him and he smiles at me . . . And his eyes moved for the first time. Not fresh or anything, but he had the look of a man with a lot of confidence and I never saw that before. Scared the life out of me. So I walk over to him and he takes my hand and leads me out to the floor . . . Everyone in the Primrose is watching. Even the band. Someone had to whisper, "Start playing," so they would begin . . . And they began. And we danced around that room. And I held my head high and my back straight as a board . . . And I looked down at the floor and up at the ceiling, but never in his eyes. I saw a professional do that once . . . His hands were so gentle. Hardly touching me at all, but I knew exactly when he wanted me to move and which way he wanted me to turn.

RUMORS

Premièred September 22, 1988
at the Old Globe Theatre, San Diego, California

Directed by Gene Saks

CAST

Chris Gorman	Christine Baranski
Ken Gorman	Mark Nelson
Claire Ganz	Jessica Walter
Lenny Ganz	Ron Leibman
Ernie Cusack	Andre Gregory
Cookie Cusack	Joyce Van Patten
Glenn Cooper	Ken Howard
Cassie Cooper	Lisa Banes
Officer Welch	Charles Brown
Officer Pudney	Cynthia Darlow

The action of the play takes place in an old Victorian house in Sneden's Landing, New York.

On the eve of Charley and Myra Brock's tenth wedding anniversary, Ken and Chris Gorman arrive to the sound of a gunshot and find Charley in his bedroom with a superficially wounded ear lobe. And wife Myra is missing. Not fully aware of the facts, but wishing to cover up potential scandal, Ken and Chris hastily contrive to obfuscate the possibility of attempted suicide. As the other party guests arrive, they are drawn into the cover-up, and, in the tradition of true farce, the evening becomes a hilarious tangle of word-play, double entendre, false rumors and accusations, and mistaken identity escalating to a fanciful climax speech by Lenny Ganz posing as Charley Brock.

From Act I:
Claire and Lenny—30-40

Lenny has heard rumors to the effect Myra Gorman is having an affair, but Claire's sources indicate otherwise—that it is her husband, Charlie, who is having clandestine amours.

LENNY. You think I don't know what you're talking about? I hear what's going on. I hear gossip, I hear rumors and I won't listen to that crap, you understand. He's my friend, she is the wife of my friend.

CLAIRE. Fine! Okay, then forget it.

LENNY. (*Looks at her.*) . . . All right. Come here. (*He walks to the extreme D.R. corner of the living room.*)

CLAIRE. What's wrong with here?

LENNY. They could hear us there. Here is better. Will you come here!

(*She crosses to him. He looks around, then to her.*)

LENNY. It's not good.

CLAIRE. What's not good?

LENNY. What I heard.

CLAIRE. What did you hear?

LENNY. Will you lower your voice?

CLAIRE. Why? You haven't said anything yet.

LENNY. All right. There's talk going around about Myra and—This hurts me. Stand on my other side. I can't turn.

(*She turns with her back to him. He moves to her other side.*)

LENNY. There's talk going around about Myra and Charley. Only no one will tell it to my face because they know I won't listen.

CLAIRE. I'll listen. Tell it to my face.

LENNY. Why do you want to hear things about our best friends? He's my best client. He trusts me. Not just about investments and taxes, but personal things.

CLAIRE. I don't do his taxes, what's the rumors?

LENNY. Jesus, you won't be satisfied until you hear, will you?

CLAIRE. I won't even *sleep* with you until I hear. What's the rumors?

LENNY. . . . . All right. Your friend Myra upstairs is having herself a little thing, okay?

CLAIRE. What kind of thing?

LENNY. Do I have to spell it out for you? A thing. A guy. A man. A fella. An affair. She's doing something with someone on the sly somewhere and it's not with Charlie.

CLAIRE. You don't know that. You only heard it. You haven't seen it.

LENNY. Of course I haven't seen it. You think they invite me to come along? What's wrong with you?

CLAIRE. You are so naïve, it's incredible. Get real, Lenny. Myra's not having anything with anybody. Your friend, Charley, however, is running up a hell of a motel bill.

LENNY. Charley? My friend, Charley? No way. Not a chance. He wouldn't even look at another woman.

CLAIRE. He may not be looking at her, but he's screwing her.

LENNY. Will you lower your voice! . . . Where did you hear this?

CLAIRE. Someone at the tennis club told me.

LENNY. *Our* tennis club?

CLAIRE. What is it, a sacred temple. People gossip there.

LENNY. Christ! Bunch of hypocrites. Sit around in their brand-new Nikes and Reeboks destroying other people's lives . . . Who told you this?

CLAIRE. I'm not going to tell you because you don't like this person anyway.

LENNY. What's the difference if I like them or not? Who told you?

CLAIRE. Carole Newman.

LENNY. CAROLE NEWMAN? I knew it, I knew it. I *hate* that woman. She's got a mouth big enough to swallow a can of tennis balls.

From Act I:
Cassie and Glenn—30-40

Rumors have been blown into the lives of Glen and Cassie Cooper, causing Cassie to wrongly accuse her husband of having an affair.

CASSIE. Don't you fucking lie to me. The whole goddamn city knows about you and that cheap little chippy bimbo.

GLENN. Will you keep it down? You're blowing this up out of all proportions. I hardly know the woman. She's on the Democratic Fund Raising Committee. I met her and her husband at two cocktail parties, for God sakes.

CASSIE. Two cocktail parties, heh?

GLENN. Yes! Two cocktail parties.

CASSIE. You think I'm stupid?

GLENN. No.

CASSIE. You think I'm blind?

GLENN. No.

CASSIE. You think I don't know what's been going on?

GLENN. Yes, because you don't.

CASSIE. I'm going to tell you something, Glenn. Are you listening?

GLENN. Don't you see my ears perking up?

CASSIE. I've known about you and Carole Newman for a year now.

GLENN. Amazing, since I only met her four months ago. Now I'm asking you to please lower you voice. That butler must be listening to everything.

CASSIE. You think I care about that a butler and a bleeding cook? My friends know about your bimbo, what do I care about domestic help?

GLENN. I don't know what's gotten into you, Cassie. Do my political ambitions bother you? Are you threatened somehow because I'm running for the Senate?

CASSIE. *State* Senate! *State* Senate! Don't make it sound like we're going to Washington. We're going to Albany. Twenty-three degrees below zero in the middle of winter Albany. You're not *Time's* Man of the Year yet, you understand, honey?

GLENN. (*Turning away.*) Oh, boy, oh, boy oh boy!

CASSIE. What was that?

GLENN. (*Deliberately.*) Oh-boy, oh-boy, oh-boy!

CASSIE. Oh, like I'm behaving badly, right? I'm the shrew witch wife who's giving you such a hard time. I'll tell you something, Mr. *State* Senator. I'm not the only one who knows what's going on. People are talking, kiddo. Trust me.

GLENN. What do you mean? You haven't said anything to anyone, have you?

CASSIE. Oh, is that what you're worried about? Your reputation? Your career? Your place in American history? You know what your place in American history will be? . . . A commemorative stamp of you and the bimbo in a motel together.

LOST in YONKERS

Premièred December 31, 1990
at the Center for the Performing Arts,
Winston-Salem, North Carolina

Directed by Gene Saks

CAST

Jay	Jamie Marsh
Arty	Danny Gerard
Eddie	Mark Blum
Bella	Mercedes Ruehl
Grandma Kurnitz	Irene Worth
Louie	Kevin Spacy
Gert	Lauren Klein

The action of the play takes place in an apartment above an ice cream-candy store in Yonkers.

Eddie Kurnitz, a deeply-in-debt widower, leaves his sons, Jay and Arty, with their grandmother until he can regain financial solvency. Grandmother Kurnitz is a disabled old-world matriarch who is looked after by her daughter Bella, a pretty woman of diminished mental capacity who also assists in managing the candy store below their apartment. Jay and Arty do their best to adapt in spite of their Grandmother's cold, unloving attitude, an attitude that has had negative psychological impact upon her children. The boys are buoyed only by the gentle kindness of Bella and letters from their father.

Bella, desperately needing to be touched and loved, finds vicarious release in movies and random forays with men. This leads to her meeting a kindred spirit in the person of John, a child-like usher at a local theater. She confides in Jay and Arty that they plan to marry, open a restaurant, and bear children. She asks for their support when she breaks the news to Grandma.

Into the mix comes younger son Louie, a street-wise man of specious character who is in hiding from persons outside the law. He is tough and cocky, the antithesis of brother Eddie, a hardened by-product of his emotionally iron mother. Louie temporarily moves into the apartment, sharing the bedroom with Jay and Arty (who find him fascinating).

Hoping to gain support for her announcement of marriage, Bella invites sister Gert to dinner. (Gert, another casualty of steel-hearted Grandma, suffers from a psychologically induced respiratory problem.) When Bella makes her plans known, she is severely criticized by Louie and is coldly-rejected by Grandma, who leaves the dinner table and retreats to her room. Bella leaves home.

When Bella returns after staying with Gert for a few days, she confronts Grandma honestly, expressing her need for love, the love that her mother has withheld. During this cathartic exchange we are taken to the core of Grandma's austerity; she has always punished herself for the premature deaths of her children Aron and Rose, and feels that her surviving them is a sin for which she deserves punishment. Bella tells Grandma that there will be no wedding because John is not willing to leave his parents and the safe confines of the darkened theater. But she has changed and—even though child-like—will never go back to being an unloved victim.

After nine months, Eddie returns to pick up his sons, who have not only survived their ordeal, they have matured as a result of dealing with it. They have grown and so has Grandma, and we sense a relaxation of her rigidity as the boys make their farewells and Bella plans for her future as a real person.

From Act I, scene i:
Arty—13-14
Jay—16

This exchange between brothers Arty and Jay opens the play. The boys wait in the living room while their father speaks to their grandmother about leaving them with her while he is away working.

JAY. I hate coming here, don't you?

ARTY. (*In front of fan.*) It's hot. I'm so hot.

JAY. I'd hate coming here if I was cool. Pop doesn't even like to come and it's his own mother . . . I was so afraid of her when I was a kid. She'd come out of that door with a limp and a cane and looked like she was gong to kill you. When I was five, I drew a picture of her and called it "Frankenstein's Grandma."

ARTY. Did she ever see it?

JAY. If she did, you'd be an only child today. Pop said she could swing her cane so fast, she could have been one of the greatest golfers in the world.

ARTY. All I remember was, I hated kissing her. If felt like putting your face on a wrinkled ice cube.

JAY. Yeah, she's cold all right. She was the only one at Mom's funeral who didn't cry . . . I wonder why Pop's talking to her for so long for.

ARTY. Because she's deaf in one ear, isn't she?

JAY. Yeah . . . Did you ever notice there's something wrong with *everyone* on Pop's side of the family? Mom used to tell me that.

ARTY. She didn't tell me. Like who?

JAY. Like all of them. Like Aunt Bella . . . She's a little—(*Points to his head.*)—you know—closed upstairs.

ARTY. I don't care. I like her. Nicer than "hot house" Grandma.

JAY. I didn't say she wasn't nice. But she's got marbles rolling around up there . . . Mom said she got that way because when she was a kid, Grandma kept hitting her in the head every time she did something stupid . . . which only made her stupider.

ARTY. (*Lays of the floor, in front of the sofa.*) She wasn't stupid at making great ice cream sodas.

JAY. Hooray! Wonderful! She's 35 years old and she can make ice cream sodas. They don't give you a high school diploma for getting the cherry on top of the whipped cream.

ARTY. She went to high school?

JAY. A little. She missed the first year because she couldn't find it.

From Act II, scene I:
Arty—13-14
Grandma—70-75

When Arty, in bed with a cold, resists drinking Grandma's curative (German mustard soup), she is tough, unsympathetic, and unrelenting.

GRANDMA. . . . (*She pulls the covers off of him.*) Come on. Out of da bed. It's enough lying around already.

ARTY. (*Pulls sheet back up.*) I'm freezing. And I'm burning up with fever. You can feel my head.

GRANDMA. You lay in bed, you get a fever. You get up and walk, da fever looks for somebody else. (*She hits the bed with her cane twice.*) Out! Out!

ARTY. (*Gets out of bed, stands and shivers.*) My mother always kept me in bed when I had a fever.

GRANDMA. (*Straightens the sheets and starts to fold the bed back into a sofa.*) You're not in your mother's house no more. (*Pointing to the chair and at the living room table.*) You sit in dat chair and you do your homework. And no funny books. And you finish dat soup. All of it.
ARTY. I tried. I can't get it down.
GRANDMA. If you eat it quick, you von't taste it.
ARTY. I would taste this if I didn't have a tongue.
GRANDMA. You listen to me. You're not fresh yet like da other one, but I see it coming. No, sir. Not in dis house . . . You live with me, you don't stay in bed two days . . . You get better qvick und you get dressed und you come downstairs und you vash up the soda fountain and you sveep up the store. I didn't ask to take care of you, but if I take care of you, you'll do vot I tell you. *Don't turn away* from me! You'll look at me! . . . You're not going to vin dis argument, I'll tell you dot right now. You understand me?
ARTY. . . . Yes.
GRANDMA. Den put da soup in your mouth right now or I do it for you.

(*He looks at her. She obviously means business. He quickly puts the soup in his mouth. He keeps it there.*)

ARTY. I can't swallow it.

(*Grandma crosses to him, pulls his head back and the soup goes down.*)

ARTY. You could drown me like that . . . Why are you so mean to me? I'm your own grandson.
GRANDMA. Dot's right. And what am I?
ARTY. What do you mean?

GRANDMA. *Vot am I?* . . . Am I a nobody?

ARTY. No. You're my grandmother.

GRANDMA. Den vere's da respect? Da respect I never got from you or your family since da day you vere born?

ARTY. You're just mad at my mother and you're taking it out on me. You don't care about your rotten soup or making me get better. You just want me to be miserable because somebody made you miserable in Germany. Even Pop said it . . . Well, it's not my fault. Take it out on Hitler, not me.

GRANDMA. Ud if you ver a boy growing up in Germany, you vould be dead by now.

ARTY. That's right. Maybe I would. And if I ate this soup, I would be just as dead. Would that make you happy? You want to be happy, Grandma? Watch! (*And he quickly eats six or seven spoonsful of the soup.*) Okay? Now you can stand there and watch me die.

GRADMA. No. You von't die. You'll be better dis afternoon. It's not so important dat you hate me, Artur . . . It's only important dat you live. (*She crosses to the door and opens it.*) Dot's something dot I could never teach your father. (*She exits.*)

From Act II, scene iii:
Bella—35
Grandma—70-75

When Bella discloses her plans to marry one of her own ilk, a child-like, forty-year-old usher, she is admonished by brother Louie and rejected by her mother. This leads to her leaving to spend a few days with her sister, Gertrude. Now she has returned, bringing with her the money she stole to finance a fantasy scheme with Johnny, her mentally challenged lover.

In this scene between her and her mother, Bella explains that even though she possesses a child-like mind, she has the desires of a

*woman, and reveals that her many sexual experiences were moti-
vated by a craving for intimacy and were substitutes for the love she
never received at home.*

GRANDMA. . . . You vant to know vot you are, Bella? . . . You're a
child. Dot's vot da doctors told me. Not crazy. Not stupid . . . A
child! . . . And dot's how I treat you. Because dot's all you understand . . . You don't need doctors. You're not sick. You don't need to
live in da Home. *Dis* is where you live. Vere you can be vatched and
taken care of . . . You'll always be a child, Bella. And in dis world,
vere dere us so much hate and sickness and death, vere nobody can
live in peace, den maybe you're better off . . . Stay a child, Bella, and
be glad dot's vot Gott made you.

BELLA. Then why did he make me look like a woman? . . . And feel
like a woman inside me? And want all the things a woman should
have? Is that what I should thank him for? Why did he do that,
Momma, when I can do everything but *think* like a woman? . . . I
know I get confused sometimes . . . and frightened. But if I'm a
child, why can't I be happy like a child? Why can't I be satisfied
with dolls instead of babies?

GRANDMA. I'm not so smart I can answer such things.

BELLA. But I *am* smart, Momma. Maybe only as smart as a child,
but some children are smarter than grown-ups. Some grown-ups I've
seen can be very stupid. And very mean.

GRANDMA. You don't haff responsibilities, Bella. And responsibilities is vot makes meanness.

BELLA. I don't want to be your responsibility. Then maybe you
won't be so mean to me.

GRANDMA. Den who vill be responsible for you? Yourself? Dot
man you ran away with? Who vants money from you? Who vants
other things from you? Gott only knows what else. Things you vould

never know about. Stay the way you are, Bella, because you don't know vot such feelings could do to you.

BELLA. Yes, I do, Momma. I know what other things you're talking about . . . Because they happened to me, Momma . . . They've happened because I *wanted* them to happen . . . You angry at me?

GRANDMA. (*Turns away, dismissing this.*) You don't know vot you're saying, Bella.

BELLA. You mean am I telling you the truth? Yes. I know what the truth is . . . Only I've been afraid to tell it to you for all these years. Gertrude knows. She's the only one . . . Do you hate me, Momma? Tell me, because I don't know if I did wrong or not.

GRANDMA. You're angry so you tell me lies. I don't vant to hear your childish lies. (*She waves Bella away.*)

BELLA. No! You *have* to listen, Momma . . . When I was in school, I let boys touch me . . . And boys that I met in the park . . . And in the movies . . . Even boys that I met here in the store . . . Nights when you were asleep, I went down and let them in . . . And just not boys, Momma . . . men too.

GRANDMA. Stop dis, Bella. You don't know vot you're saying . . . You dream these things in your head.

BELLA. I needed somebody to touch me, Momma. Somebody to hold me. To tell me I was pretty . . . *You* never told me that. Some even told me they loved me but I never believed them because I knew what they wanted from me . . . Except John. He *did* love me. Because he understood me. Because he was like me. He was the only one I ever felt safe with. And I thought maybe for the first time I *could* be happy . . . That's why I ran away. I even brought the five thousand dollars to give to him for the restaurant. Then maybe he'd find the courage to leave home too.

JAKE'S WOMEN

Premièred March 24, 1992 at the
Neil Simon Theatre, New York City

Directed by Gene Saks

CAST

Jake	Alan Alda
Maggie	Helen Shaver
Karen	Brenda Vaccaro
Molly (at 12)	Genia Michaela
Molly (at 21)	Tracy Pollan
Edith	Joyce Van Patten
Julie	Kate Burton
Sheila	Talia Balsam

The action of the play takes place in Jake's apartment in Soho and in his mind.

Jake, a writer, immerses himself in the world of fiction as a way of avoiding honest interaction and expressing real feelings. He is more comfortable facing his word processor than facing life's realties. When a marital crisis arises, he turns to the comfortable world of his creative imagination because it affords him a means of controlling events and outcomes. Through a mixture of flashbacks, fantasies and reality, we meet Jake's women: his first wife, Julie, who was tragically killed in an automobile accident; his daughter, Molly, as both a juvenile and an adult; his abrasive analyst, Edith; his authoritative sister; Karen, his current wife Maggie, who is asking for a six-months separation; and a prospective third wife, Shelia.

The play is an intricate study of a person haunted by an inability to relinquish control, face truth, and come to terms with honest feelings.

From Act I:
Jake—45-55
Karen—35-45

After an imaginary interlude with his wife, Maggie, during which he recalls their first meeting, Jake, the creative writer, prepares for her actual return and a confrontation regarding their marital problems by having an imaginary, scripted conversation with his sister, Karen.

JAKE. I think Maggie's getting ready to leave me.
KAREN. Don't tell me. Oh, my God, no. Why? What happened?
JAKE. A lot of things that never should have happened.
KAREN. Alright, don't jump to conclusions . . . Don't try to guess what's going on in someone else's mind. I used to worry that Harry was going to leave me too.
JAKE. But he *did* leave you.
KAREN. Because I kept saying, "You're going to leave me one day, I know it." I drove him crazy . . . Besides, we had big problems. You and Maggie had eight good years together. She loves you, that I would bet my life on.
JAKE. She's seeing another man.
KAREN. I'm such a bad judge of character. Are you positive, Jake?

JAKE. It's someone new in her office. I don't know if he means something to her of it's just a symptom of what's wrong with us.

KAREN. What *is* wrong with you?

JAKE. Something stopped.

KAREN. I am so depressed. Is there something wrong with our family, Jake? Mom got divorced. Pop got divorced. I got divorced. Now you're getting divorced.

JAKE. Mom and Pop are one divorce. And I'm not divorced yet. Don't make it an epidemic, Karen.

KAREN. Have you been seeing anyone?

JAKE. Me? No.

KAREN. You haven't been seeing another woman?

JAKE. Didn't I just say so?

KAREN. Who's the other woman?

JAKE. An actress, about a year ago. It only lasted about three weeks.

KAREN. You mean, if it's under a month, it's not an affair? Every man in America is looking for a calendar like that.

JAKE. I expected you to be supportive.

KAREN. No, you expected me to say what you want to hear. Alright, how's this? . . . "You're entitled to an affair. You work hard. It would kill Momma to hear but she's dead anyway so what do *you* care?"

JAKE. Karen, I don't need you to make me feel guilty.

KAREN. Yes, you do. I don't mind. I'm not working anyway . . . So tell me, are you still seeing this tramp?

JAKE. She's not a tramp . . . No. It's over. The truth is, I love Maggie more now than I ever have in my life. I don't want to lose her, Karen. If I lose here, I lose everything.

KAREN. Oh Jake, Jake. You're so dependent on women. I've always known that. I wish I could hold you right now. I want to grab you in my arms the way Momma did and make you feel wonderful and safe and loved. But you have me, Jake. You can count on me . . .

This is another good speech. Give me more like this. This is a woman you could like.

JAKE. Everyone likes you, Karen.

KAREN. So why can't I make a marriage work? Don't end up alone like me, Jake. I live in the movies, night after night, and you can't be happy living in a popcorn world . . . No! See that's crappy dialogue. You're getting even with me now for the crack about Momma.

JAKE. I'm sorry. I'll fax you the rewrites tomorrow, okay?

KAREN. Does that mean I'm going?

JAKE. (*Turns his head.*) No. I hear Maggie coming up the stairs. Stay a few minutes.

KAREN. I'm in you head. How am I going to get out, when you sneeze?

From Act II:
Maggie—35-40
Jake—45-55

After six months of separation, Maggie has come to see Jake. She still loves him, but needs assurance that he is capable of getting in touch with real feelings and facing reality.

JAKE. . . . So what brings you here?

MAGGIE. I just wanted to see you. To talk to you.

JAKE. I sense something important is about to be said.

MAGGIE. I think the man I'm going to have dinner with tonight is going to propose to me.

JAKE. I see. Well, that qualifies as important. Probably in the same category as "My house is on fire" . . . How do you feel about it?

MAGGIE. I scared I might say yes.

JAKE. Who isn't? . . . And what's the frightening part?

MAGGIE. That it would be over with us.

JAKE. Well, it would certainly slow us down . . . I don't suppose I could come along and coach you? . . . No . . . What does he do?

MAGGIE. He listens to me. He pays attention.

JAKE. You mean for a living?

MAGGIE. Jesus!

JAKE. What?

MAGGIE. I'm sitting here telling you that in twenty minutes I may be making the biggest decision of my life and I don't feel any concern from you or any interest in my life unless it's connected to you.

JAKE. I'm concerned. If you got sick, I would worry. If you got married, I'd be pissed . . . Since I care for you, that seems pretty reasonable to me.

MAGGIE. I still care for you too, Jake. But it doesn't depend on our getting together or not.

JAKE. Am I dense because I'm not rooting for the other guy to get the girl?

MAGGIE. No matter what we talk about, it always seems to come out like a story conference.

JAKE. Well, if it is, I never seem to get past the editor. Christ, Maggie, if we're just going to pick up where we left off six months ago, you should have gone straight to dinner.

MAGGIE. I was hoping that things might have changed since six months ago.

JAKE. (*Shrugs.*) They have. You found a guy who listens better than I do.

MAGGIE. Don't listen to the words, Jake. Listen to the feelings. There's pain going on here. Your pain and mine. And we can't get anywhere until we get in touch with those feelings. We're like two people reaching out for each other with both hands tied behind our backs.

JAKE. (*Confused.*) Why can't I understand your concept of getting in touch with pain? I don't think I just speak words. I speak feelings and emotions. I care. I love. I'm miserable. I'm angry. I'm desperate. I'm hopeful and mostly I'm confused. Am I getting close?

MAGGIE. Yes, Jake. You're getting close.

JAKE. Thank God. Tell me what I did so I can hold on to it.

MAGGIE. I think part of you is standing right there in front of me, listening and talking to me . . . But there's that other part of you. The writer. The observer who's standing up there in his office, right now, watching and observing the two of us, detached as hell, and *he's* the one who's getting in our way, Jake. He's the one who's not involved in our problem. He's a voyeur. A manipulator. And unless you can let go of him and trust yourself, Jake, trust how you feel and not what he judges to be the truth, then you'll never feel safe with me or anyone . . . And that would be such a loss . . .

JAKE. Jesus, Maggie, You make me feel so isolated. So inhuman.

MAGGIE. No. I think you're alone. I think you put yourself there a long time ago because it feels safe to you. All that I'm asking is that you come out of your hiding place and join the rest of us. There's a lot of people out here who love you, Jake. Trust it.

JAKE. (*He's hoping to explain.*) I don't observe because I chose to. I'm not alone because I prefer it. I'm not a writer because I'm good at it . . . I write to survive. It's the only thing that doesn't reject me. My characters are the only ones I know who love me unconditionally, because I give them life. Do you love me unconditionally, Maggie?

MAGGIE. I'm not that selfless. And you didn't give me life, Jake. My mother did. And I like you much better than I like her.

JAKE. Do you? Funny, you look about ten miles away from where I sit.

MAGGIE. No, Jake. I think we're so close. I swear. I think we're only an inch or two apart.

JAKE. What's wrong with that? Most couples I know have the Grand Canyon between them and they don't even notice.

MAGGIE. I notice. But I want more than that for us.

JAKE. I mean this in all sincerity. I wish I were as smart as you.

MAGGIE. I wasn't this smart before I married you. You made me think. You made me observe.

JAKE. So why doesn't your observer run off with *my* observer and you and I can stay here?

MAGGIE. Okay. If you want me to stay, I'll stay. If you want me to come back, I'll come back,

JAKE. (*Smiles.*) You're tricky, you really are. You know I'd grab that in a minute. But you're also smart enough to know that I'm smart enough to know it wouldn't work. That I know you're right. That until I cross those two inches, until I can understand the *concept* of those two inches, we'd always be in trouble.

MAGGIE. You know something, Jake. Even though we've just been pretty tough on each other, this is one of the best talks we've ever had.

JAKE. Really? I hated it. I grew up seeing movies where saying "I love you" was a happy ending.

MAGGIE. Maybe it will be. Once we realize this isn't a movie . . . I'm late for dinner.

JAKE. You're not really going to say "Yes" to him tonight, are you? I mean, is this guy only a quarter of an inch away from you or what?

MAGGIE. No, I'm not going to say yes . . . I'm going to wait till I hear from you.

JAKE. Oh, you're just going to leave me walking around here all day with a tape measure? What are you hoping is going to happen?

MAGGIE. A catharsis! A bolt of lighting! A miracle!

JAKE. Jesus, now I have to be the Messiah.

MAGGIE. No, I'll just settle for Jake . . . So long, Jake. (She *goes.*)

LAUGHTER on the 23RD FLOOR

Premièred November 22, 1993
at the Richard Rodgers Theatre, New York City

Directed by Jerry Zaks

CAST

Lucas	Stephen Mailer
Milt	Lewis. J. Stadlen
Val	Mark Linn-Baker
Brian	J. K. Simmons
Kenny	John Slattery
Carol	Randy Graff
Max Prince	Nathan Lane
Helen	Betty Schram
Ira	Roy Orbach

The action of the play takes place in an office of the 23rd floor of a building on 57th Street, New York City.

This autobiographical play chronicles events during Neil Simon's stint as a writer for *Your Shows of Shows* starring Sid Caesar. Arguably the best comedy/variety TV program of all time, the show was spearheaded by Caesar's comic genius backed the stellar writing of Simon and writers such as Larry Gelbart and Mel Brooks.

Lucas (Simon) is a new writer on the show. Shy and unprepossessing, he initially finds it difficult to keep pace with the madcap behavior and sarcastic banter of the other writers. Max (Caesar), a man both feared and respected by his writers, is a bigger-than life, temperamental, driven genius given to fits of paranoia and explosive tantrums. He is also a demanding workaholic who over-indulges in food, booze and tranquilizers—his pallet is large and he paints broadly on it. In spite of this, he is a motivating optimist who protects his writers, and is uncompromising with respect to the show's excellence.

Set in 1953, during the time Joe McCarthy is spreading "Commie" hysteria, the play deals with Max's ongoing battle with NBC regarding the show's length and level of sophistication. The network feels the show is too long and going over the heads of the general populous. When the show is cut to one hour, Max marshals his writers, demanding they maintain their high level of satirical material—he is a fighter who will not sacrifice quality nor talk down to his viewing audience. (The story of the play is propelled by the rapier-wit dialogue and madcap antics of its characters.)

In the concluding scene—on Christmas Eve—when Max calls his staff together to tell them the show has been cancelled, he announces the cancellation as a victory—they have won because they are now free to pursue greater, more lucrative careers. Even in defeat he is optimistic.

From Act I:
Lucas—25
Milt—25-30

Lucas is alone in the writers room. He has been on the job only two weeks. He tends to be shy and withdrawn and is nervous about his chances of surviving his four-week trial. Then Milt enters. He is flamboyant, cocky, self-assured and uplifting.

(*The door opens. Milt Fields, another writer, enters. He wears a black cape over a sports jacket, a bow tie and a black beret on his head.*)

MILT. (*In the doorway.*) I did it. Broke every record on the Henry Hudson Parkway. Door to door, Scarsdale to 57th Street, twenty-eight minutes, twelve seconds, made every light . . . Can you imagine if I had a car? (*Crossing to Lucas.*) Ba-dum-bum. How you doing, Arnie?

LUCAS. Fine. It's Lucas.

MILT. It's not Arnie?

LUCAS. No.

MILT. I called you Arnie all last week, you never said a word.

LUCAS. I didn't know you were talking to me.

MILT. You're going to have to learn to speak up, kid. Otherwise these killers'll eat you alive. (*He throws his cape.*) Hang this up, will ya? Be careful with it. It's an antique.

LUCAS. (*Touches it.*) Feels nice. Where'd you get it?

MILT. I took it off a dead bullfighter in Spain. What do I know? A junk shop. But it's got style, class. I got a flair for dressing, no?

LUCAS. A flair? You got a rocket. Where'd you get the beret?

MILT. The beret is legitimate. Got it in Paris. The last one sold.

LUCAS. The last one in Paris?

MILT. MGM bought 'em all up for Gene Kelly movies.

(*Lucas nods.*)

MILT. Look, he believes me. What do I know about berets? And I look like a putz in this. So why would I wear it?

LUCAS. Why?

MILT. Because people notice it. Look at me without a beret. (*He takes it off.*) Invisible, right. A nothing. Who is he? But watch. (*He puts beret back on.*) Now I'm someone. A diplomat. A traveler. Maybe I know Ernest Hemingway. I go to French Movies, laugh at the jokes, (*He laughs*) don't understand a fucking word they're saying, but people come over on the way out. "You like the picture?" "Eh, comme ci, comme ça." I don't even understand *that* but I get attention. I'm unique, right?

LUCAS. Well . . .

MILT. What am I, good looking? No. Am I smart? Eh. Am I funny? Yes. But compared to the comic minds in this room, I'm Herbert Hoover's kitchen soup help . . . So I wear yellow suede shoes on Christmas and a cowboy hat on Yom Kippur. And when I walk in here, Max Prince laughs. And if Max Prince laughs, my kids eat this week.

LUCAS. Max didn't talk to me once last week.

MILT. Alright. I'll rent you the beret. Fifty bucks a week. If he picks up your option, seventy-five.

LUCAS. No, that's okay.

MILT. (*Hands him beret.*) Here. It's gift. (*He pulls a red one from one pocket and a green one from the other pocket.*) I'm up to my ass in berets.

LUCAS. (*Smiles.*) And you don't think you're funny?

MILT. (*Putting away the red and green berets.*) Cheap! Cheap laughs! These guys are Tiffany's. I'm a wholesaler. (*Crossing to the bagel table.*) What they have in quality, I make up in quantity. Bulk, volume, that's my humor. Where's the onion rolls? It's in my contract. My agent negotiated for onion rolls.

LUCAS. (*Points.*) Isn't that one?

MILT. (*Picks up a small dark roll.*) This? This is a Jewish hockey puck. Smell it. Does that smell like an onion roll?

LUCAS. I can't smell it. I have a cold. I could listen to it if you want.

MILT. (*He grabs the beret from Lucas.*) You're funny, Arnie. You're too quiet, but you're funny. Don't be *too* funny. I have a wife and two kids to support. It's murder on my mistress.

BOTH. (*Together.*) Ba-dum-bum.

MILT. You'll be alright.

From Act I:
Max—30-35
Milt—25-30
Brian—25-30
Val—30-35
Carol—25-30
Kenny—25-30

When the writer's express their concern for Max's health, he announces that his anxiety and sleeplessness are due to his conflicts with NBC who want him to cut the show to an hour and dumb down its content

MAX. (*Holds his head.*) I can't remember anything. I think somebody's drugging me, I swear to God.

VAL. Well, Max, that brings up a another delicate subject.

MAX. I fell asleep the other night with my eyes open. I thought I was dreaming about the ceiling.

VAL. In the first place, Max, you know we all love you.

MAX. Sometimes I go in the kitchen in the middle of the night, get a hammer and smash walnuts. Why would I do that?

KENNY. I think Freud says that's a symptom of fear.

MAX. Why? I'm not afraid of walnuts . . . You want to hear the worst part?

CAROL. I thought we did, Max.

MAX. When I eat, I can't tell the difference between steak and fish anymore. Why is that? (*He is near tears.*)

BRIAN. Where did they catch your steak, Max?

(*Max glares at Brian. Brian looks away.*)

MAX. (*To Val.*) What was the delicate subject?

VAL. Well, it's just that we feel for your own good, Max, for your own health, for your family's well being . . .

MAX. I don't want to hear my fortune. I just want to hear the delicate subject.

KENNY. We don't think those pills you take before you leave here at night are good for your, Max.

MAX. (*Confused.*) What pills?

VAL. The pills, Max. That you take before you go home.

MAX. I take pills? What are your talking about? Those tranquilizers? They're prescription. Two little pills.

KENNY. *Little pills?* We could play nine innings of soft ball with one pill.

MAX. I hardly take them. Once a week.

BRIAN. You take them once a week every night, Max.

MAX. They're harmless. Carol, remember you weren't feeling well one night? I gave you half a pill. Did anything happen?

CAROL. I don't remember. I slept for nine days.

KENNY. It's just not the pills. It's the four jiggers of Scotch you take to wash them down. Pills and liquor don't mix, Max. Or max, Mix, however you want.

MAX. I gotta sleep. If I don't sleep, who's gonna protect my family from them?

CAROL. NBC is threatening your family?

MAX. They're threatening my show. My show is my life. If they threaten my life, they threaten my family. You want to hear the letter they sent me? You want to know what they said, word for word for word?

MILT. Go ahead, Max. The doors are still closed.

MAX. (*Leans back in his chair, looks at his cigar.*) . . . They said . . . "Give the people shit."

(*The all look at each other.*)

CAROL. The President of NBC said that?

MAX. You heard me. "Give the people shit."

BRIAN. You mean as a gift?

CAROL. Why would he say that, Max?

MAX. Because—they can make money on shit. A pot full. Drive up to Connecticut, they got big Tudor shit houses wherever you look, that's why they invented television. They put shit on for people to watch, they advertise shit, the people run out and buy shit, the kids break the shit, so they buy them more shit and the shit moguls go to France in the summer and the poor people stay here and watch more shit . . . That's why I got a letter saying, "Give the people shit."

MILT. (*Aside to Carol.*) Isn't that what Marie Antoinette said?

CAROL. (*Swatting Milt.*) Why do you always talk to *me?* Annoy somebody else once in a while.

KENNY. Let me take a whack at this. For four years in a row we sweep the Emmy Awards. Every critic in the country loves us. But suddenly television is expanding. They're going into the midwest, the south. Different kinds of audience. They want to watch quiz shows, bowling, wrestling, right?

MAX. (*Nods.*) If you got shit, shovel it over.

KENNY. So they want to cut us to an hour. Don't make the shows too esoteric. Too smart. Don't do take-offs on Japanese movies, Italian movies.

MAX. Feed a horse hay, what are you going to get?

CAROL. You don't even have to say it, Max.

KENNY. So it's not only cutting the half hour, it's the kind of show they want us to do?

VAL. Can't we talk to them, Max?

MAX. Talk? No! No talk! Fight! We fight them on the sea, we fight them on the beaches. Or we'll get the bastards in an alley in Brooklyn somewhere. Remember what Churchill said? "Never have so many given so much for so long for so little for so few for so seldom" . . .

LONDON SUITE

Premièred October 12, 1994
at the Seattle Repertory Theatre, Seattle, Washington

Directed by Daniel Sullivan

CAST
"Settling Accounts"

Brian   Jeffery Joney
Billy   Paxton Whitehead

CAST
"Going Home"

Lauren   Kate Burton
Mrs. Semple   Carole Shelley

London Suite is comprised of four one-act plays whose action takes place in a fashionable hotel in London, England.

"Settling Accounts"

An author has abducted his long-time, dishonest business manager as he was about to abscond with the remnants of his money, and is holding him at gun point in the hotel. He is drunk, vindictive, and not buying his frightened hostage's fanciful lies.

From Scene i:
Brian and Billy—50

BILLY. Brian, my dear friend, Brian. What can I say? I feel so ashamed.

BRIAN. Yes, I can see that. I have just one minor question for you. (Bill *looks up.*) How many of us did you steal from?. . . Half? . . . Ten? . . . Five? . . . How many, Billy?

BILLY. . . . Just you.

BRIAN. Just *me?* . . . Just *me?* . . . Not *them?* Not the *others?* . . . None of your five and ten million pound members of your bloody bleeding Grand Masters sterling silver inner sanctum money movers? Just me! (*Right in* Bill's *face.*) You whining, worthless piece of treacherous crud! I don't need a gun to kill you. I'll do it with a bloody *fruit fork,* you bastard! (*He grabs fruit fork from bowl of fruit, grabs* Bill *by his collar and holds the fork above him.*) Why *me?* . . . Why was *I* the one you picked?

BILLY. Because you were the only one who didn't ask questions! (Brian *is stunned; he releases* Bill.) Do you know why all my other clients are so wealthy, Brian? They pay attention. They ask questions. They could look at their portfolios and know if a digit or a decimal point was in the wrong place. They watched their money like hawks. You never knew where the Goddamn *nest* was. For two months I slipped one egg after another from under your wings. You were *begging* me to rob you, don't you see that? The great writer looking down his nose at the mere mention of money, blinding himself to his responsibility of watching over it . . . It takes two to steal, Brian. One to take and one to give.

BRIAN. (*Looks at him.*) Do I have *anything* left?

BILLY. . . . No.

BRIAN. Not even a little account? One you might have forgotten about?

BILLY. No. I got it all.

BRIAN. All of it? All two million one hundred thousand pounds?

BILLY. Two million six hundred and twelve thousand pounds. You didn't even know what you had, did you? My four-year-old grandson could steal from you without your knowing.

BRIAN. Started training him early, have you? Well, it's getting past your dead time. (*He takes out the gun, grabs* Bill *by the collar.*)

"Going Home"

On their last evening in London, Lauren, a caring daughter, insists her widowed mother date a charming, wealthy Scotsman she met on their flight over. She feels her mother should get on with her life and establish a relationship.

When her mother returns to the hotel after the date, Lauren learns that the Scot has a physiological resistance to marriage and, furthermore, her mother is already involved in a loving relationship at home.

From Scene iii:
Lauren—30-35
Mother—55-60

LAUREN. Goodnight. (*The Mother crosses into bedroom, takes off her jacket, then sits on the edge of the bed, lost in thought. On sofa,*

Lauren *calls out.*) You want me to leave a wake-up call? (*A moment.*) Mom?

(*The* Mother *gets up and walks slowly into the living room, stands in the doorway.*)

MOTHER. Laurie . . . can you take a few more minutes?
LAUREN. You mean there's more?
MOTHER. Yes.
LAURAN. Of course.

(*The* Mother *crosses back into the living room.*)

MOTHER. You were right about what you said earlier tonight. I do lean a lot on you and Andy and the baby. It's been hard for me without your father, but as you said, it has been *six* years.
LAUREN. Mom, if I pushed you too hard tonight, I am so—
MOTHER. No, no. It's alright. I went out tonight to test the waters. What if it turned out to be wonderful? What if I really ended up in Scotland? Married, living out my life there? How would you feel?
LAUREN. If you were happy, I would be too. I'd miss you but we'd work it out . . . What is it, Mom?
MOTHER. . . . There *is* a man in my life. For about a year and a half now. He lives about an hour from me. I've managed to keep it quiet. You never met him, but your dad knew him. We all used to play golf together. Dad liked him a lot.
LAUREN. And you thought I wouldn't approve? Why couldn't you tell me?
MOTHER. . . . He's married.
LAUREN. Oh . . . well, that *is* a problem, isn't it? . . . Does his wife know?

MOTHER. She had a stroke about three years ago. She's bed ridden. The doctors said she'd never really be . . . *never* be there for him anymore, but that she could go on living for years . . .

LAUREN. Oh, God, Mom. I'm so sorry.

MOTHER. For her. For him . . . They can't help it, but I've got no choice . . . Do you think I'm wrong? Seeing him, I mean.

LAUREN. No. How could I?

MOTHER. He's a wonderful man. It's more a friendship than an affair, but also more than a friendship . . .

LAUREN. Is it enough for you, Mom? The way it is?

MOTHER. I think so. I don't know how I'd handle a full out relationship yet. I'd have to build up to it.

LAUREN. You will . . . (*The* Mother *tries to hold back her tears.*) Come on, it's been a long night.

(Lauren *starts for the bedroom. The* Mother *starts to follow.*)

MOTHER. You know . . .

LAUREN. What?

MOTHER. Somehow . . . I had a feeling you knew this all along . . . Don't tell me if you did. If you knew, just say, "Let's go to bed, Mom."

LAUREN. If I knew, why wouldn't I have told you?

MOTHER. To protect me. To honor my secret. Because that's what a loving daughter would do.

LAUREN. (*Looks at her, smiles.*) Let's go to bed, Mom.

(Lauren *crosses into bedroom.* Mother *stands there, then she starts into bedroom . . . WE FADE TO BLACK.*)

PROPOSALS

Premièred November 6, 1997
at the Broadhurst Theatre, New York City

Directed by Joe Mantello

CAST

Clemma Diggins	L. Scott Caldwell
Burt Hines	Dick Latessa
Josie Hines	Suzanne Cryer
Ken Norman	Reg Rogers
Ray Dolenz	Matt Lestscher
Annie Robbins	Kelly Bishop
Vinnie Bavasi	Peter Rini
Sammii	Kate Finneran
Lewis Barnett	Mel Winkler

The action of the play takes place near a resort in the Pocono Mountains, Pennsylvania.

The final day a family is together is complicated by a convergence of personalities.

This memory piece is unfolded by Clemma Diggins, housekeeper for recovering heart attack patient, Burt Hines. Her recollection brings to life a summer's day in 1953 when personalities overlap, resulting in conflict, discovery, and resolution: Burt eagerly anticipates the arrival of his ex-wife, Annie, who he still loves; his daughter, Josie, has just broken her engagement to an intense Harvard law student, Kenny, and still carries a torch for his buddy, Ray, with whom she had a brief affair; Clemma is dreading a visit from, Lewis, the husband who deserted her seven years before; Ray appears on the scene with Sammii, a gorgeous model who is not so gorgeous in the smarts department; Vinnie, a young gangster given to malapropisms, arrives unannounced to see Josie with whom he had once danced while she was in Miami.

From Act I, scene i:
Josie and Kenny—20-25

Josie and Kenny have emerged from the woods where she has just told him their wedding is off. He is an Ivy League type and very depressed. Josie is athletic, vital, full of energy. She is carrying a stick.

JOSIE. (*To* Kenny.) You okay?
KENNY. Okay? . . . Oh, yeah . . . Yes . . . I'm okay . . . I'm fine . . . I really am . . . No, I'm not okay . . . I will be . . . One day.
JOSIE. (*Nods. Doesn't know what to say.*) . . . Kenny?
KENNY. What?
JOSIE. Would you like a beer?
KENNY. Instead of getting married? No . . .
JOSIE. Well, I think that's what I need right now.

(Josie *looks at him, wanting to say something. She can't, turns and goes into the house.* Kenny *picks up her stick, looks at it, swishes it a couple of times, then in a quick fury, he breaks the stick over his knee, then he breaks it again and tosses the pieces into the woods.* Josie *comes out with a bottle of beer. She drinks from it.*)

JOSIE. God, I really love beer. One day, I'm going to get so fat from drinking this.

KENNY. Yeah, right.

JOSIE. No. I am. I'm going to get big fat hips like I'm carrying tennis balls in my pockets. And big jowls hanging down. And little piggy eyes and nubby knees and I'm going to wear Hawaiian dresses the rest of my life.

KENNY. Is that what you want me to think, Josie? That you're going to blow up to two hundred and eighty pounds? . . . Fine with me. Let's get married and I'll buy bigger furniture.

JOSIE. (*Dismisses it, looks around.*) Where's my stick? Did you see my stick?

KENNY. No.

JOSIE. Really? I left it right here.

KENNY. I broke it.

JOSIE. You broke my stick? . . . Why?

KENNY. Because it was *my* time to break something.

JOSIE. Oh. It's okay. I don't blame you for hating me.

KENNY. *Hate* you? I love you. I loved you from the first time I saw you.

JOSIE. What I meant is, I'm the one who broke off the engagement and for that, you have every right to hate me.

KENNY. Sorry to disappoint you, but I don't . . . I hate my *life*. I hate the *world*. I hate *mankind*. I hate every living creature that crawls and flies, but I'm not through loving you yet.

(Josie *reaches out and rubs the top of his hand.*)

JOSIE. Kenny, the one thing I hope we'll always be—

KENNY. PLEASE! Don't say friends . . . I have no interest in the smile or scent of my friends.

JOSIE. I'm sorry.

KENNY. The thing is, if you wanted to break it off, why did you wait so long?

JOSIE. I didn't. I wrote you a letter two months ago at school.

KENNY. That wasn't a letter. That as a poem. Where did it say, "Break off the engagement?"

JOSIE. It said it in the poetry. In the imagery. In the metaphors. Did you read it?

KENNY. Yes. "Brazen Idols, black damask cheek. Catatonic smiles who cannot speak.?" . . . That's how you break off with Shelly and Keats. I'm a law student.

JOSIE. I wrote other letters but never sent them. I thought it was too cowardly not to say it face to face.

KENNY. Except it wasn't face to face. You were standing behind me when you poked me with a stick. "Would you mind awfully, Ken, if we don't get married?" . . . Poke poke . . . "Would I mind awfully?" . . . What's that supposed to be, polite? Did your mother teach you, "whenever breaking off an engagement, always stand behind the gentleman and poke him gently with a stick and say, "Would you mind awfully?" . . . Poke poke.

JOSIE. I'm sorry. It just came out.

KENNY. No, no. I saw you looking for a stick. Why a stick?

JOSIE. I was trying to get you attention.

KENNY. *"Would you mind awfully if we didn't get married?"* got *my attention* . . . You didn't *need* a stick . . . (*He rubs his neck.*)

JOSIE. It was a bad choice.

KENNY. Why today Josie? Why didn't you tell me before?

JOSIE. I'm not sure. I guess I was waiting until I was absolutely clear that getting married would be a big mistake for us . . . God, this is hard, Kenny. I care for you. I do. I really have strong feelings for you.

KENNY. I just don't know why you said yes. If you meant "no," how could you have said "yes?"

JOSIE. Because it seemed right at the time. I thought you were wonderful, Kenny. I still do. You're so smart. So involved with things. Political things. Causes. Things you care about. And you have such great parents . . . And your mother is incredible. I'm closer to her than I am to my own mother. And I just got swept up by it all . . . So when you suddenly said while we were dancing at the Democratic Convention, "Lets' get engaged," I thought, "Swell. What a great guy to be engaged to" . . . I guess I never really thought about it leading up to marriage.

KENNY. What did you *think* it would lead up to? More Democratic Conventions?

JOSIE. I just loved being with you. Until I finally realized something was wrong. I was enjoying living *your* life. I was forgetting about living mine.

KENNY. Then forget mine. It's not important. I can live mine in my spare time.

JOSIE. . . . When my mother left my father, he was devastated. He loved her. He still does. I realize that's not the same because they had twenty-one years together . . . But even with all that, he found that time heals. That you move on. And he's learned to accept that.

KENNY. Gee, that story certainly perked me up. So now I know what I have to look forward to . . . Acceptance.

JOSIE. No. You have your *life* to look forward to.

KENNY. Can't you just hold off your decision until the end of the summer?

JOSIE. Nothing will change.

KENNY. I wish I could have been born your brother.

JOSIE. Why?

KENNY. So I'd always be around you . . . but if I was your brother and you loved me the way I wanted you to, that would be really sick . . . so forget that one.

JOSIE. I do love you. In my own way.

(Josie *puts her arms around* Kenny, *hugs him.*)

KENNY. If I had one wish in the world, I would—(*He catches himself about to cry, walks away.*) . . . I wasn't' crying. I'm saving that for the trip back home.

JOSIE. You want me to drive you home?

KENNY. Oh. The final humiliation. Drop me off in front of my mother who's writing out the invitations?

JOSIE. What are you going to tell her?

KENNY. I'll have my father tell her. She never listens to what he says anyway. (*He looks at her.*) I'll just love you for another few months . . . and then I'll try to cut down. (*He starts to go.*)

JOSIE. Kenny, wait. (*He turns, looks at her.*) I have to give our ring back. (*Starts to loosen it*)

KENNY. No! Don't! . . . Not while I'm watching.

From Act I, scene iii:
Josie—20-25
Annie—45-50

Annie, Burt's ex-wife, has just arrived. She is attractive, smartly dressed, and still has her trim figure. But her relationship with her daughter, Josie, is strained because Josie has never forgiven her for leaving her father. Here, shortly after her arrival, when she suggests the events of the day may be to stressful for Burt's "condition," Josie's hostility surfaces, triggering the following exchange:

ANNIE. Don't you think this is a lot for him to deal with? In his condition.

JOSIE. Condition?

ANNIE. You know what I'm talking about. His health.

JOSIE. Oh. Well, his health is lousy but his condition is fine. He's having a good summer. Obviously not as good as other summers but he fishes a little and we walk some and he laughs a lot. He just likes being with his family. Me and Clemma.

(Annie *turns, walks away.*)

ANNIE. Josie, if you want to hurt me, I'll meet you in the city and you can do it there. But not here. And not today. Give your father this weekend, will you?

JOSIE. I give him every weekend . . . But, yes, this is a special weekend. Because you're here. He still loves you, you know. Well, of course you do . . . And he'll have you until tomorrow afternoon. And then you'll fly off to Paris or Rome or where ever your husband is waiting for you. So I hope you'll understand if I get upset when you start to talk to me about his condition.

ANNIE. I understand perfectly. And I am not asking for understanding when I tell you I never walked away from this situation Scot free. I pay for it everyday of my life. Especially the days when I talk to you. That is *my* condition. And I will deal with it in my own way. What bothers me is our condition, our relationship. I am still part of *your* family. And I don't know how to get back in. I need some help from you. Do you know how we can do that?

JOSIE. No.

ANNIE. Are you saying you're turning your back on me?

JOSIE. No. I'm saying it sincerely. I hate what's happening between us. But I'm telling you I don't know how to make it better.

ANNIE. Well, then, we'll have to find a way, won't we? . . . I'm going in. I need to wash off seventeen hours of TWA.

From Act II, scene ii:
Clemma—40-50
Lewis—45-55

Clemma's husband, Lewis, blinded in one eye and seriously arthritic, has shown up unexpectedly after an absence of seven years. He has come with hopes for reconciliation and to explain the reasons behind his leaving years before. Initially cool, Clemma warms to him ever so slightly, offers him a slice of pie. The ensuing dialogue uncovers guilty secrets destructive to their relationship and reveals a mutual caring.

LEWIS. Clemma . . . You are the only woman that I want.
CLEMMA. Since when? What's so special about me, Lewis, that you have to see once every seven years?
LEWIS. Meanin' why did I up and leave in the first place? . . . Well, lately I've been thinkin' about that.
CLEMMA. It just come up *lately,* I ain't interested.
LEWIS. Will you let me *talk,* Clemma? . . . You always had to have the last word, didn't you? A man doesn't like to hear that. I never did.
CLEMMA. Alright . . . Go on . . . Say what's on your mind.

(Clemma *sits opposite* Lewis.)

LEWIS. . . . I knew what it meant to you to be without a child. And when the doctor told you you'd never be able to have your own, I thought it was my fault. I thought that time we had a scuffle on the stairs when you found out some bad things, that I killed every baby you could ever have. But you looked at the doctor and said, "Well, I still got my Lewis so God must still love me anyways." . . . (Lewis *looks at* Clemma. *Her eyes move away at the memory of that mo-*

ment.) I have never felt guilt like that, in all my life. And it was that guilt that drove me away, Clemma. Because I had no call gettin' so much love from such a good woman.

CLEMMA. That's right. You didn't . . . But there was somethin' I never told you . . . I knew I could never have a child long before I fell down those stairs. Long before I met you. And I didn't tell you 'bout it after the accident, 'cause I thought your guilt would keep you from ever leaving me . . . well, we was both wrong, wasn't we?

LEWIS. Yes . . . If you kept that from me for so long, why you telling it to me now?

CLEMMA. Because it was time to unload something that was sittin' heavy on my conscience. Just 'cause you was a sinner, Lewis, didn't mean I was a saint.

LEWIS. You don't have to be so harsh on yourself, Clemma.

CLEMMA. Yes, I do. 'Cause I ain't through accusin' you yet . . . The truth is, it wasn't your guilt that drove you away. You just had a roving eye for other women . . . And the Lord fixed that, didn't he?

LEWIS. I guess he did.

CLEMMA. (*Shakes her head.*) . . . What a pair of fools and liars we were, Lewis.

LEWIS. Ain't that the truth.

CLEMMA. But maybe it was all God's plan. Maybe I was meant to lose you and find someone like Josie to fill my life.

LEWIS. Well, if it was God's plan, maybe He ain't finished yet.

CLEMMA. Meanin' what?

LEWIS. Well, Josie may be ready to move on with her own life. So maybe the plan was for me to reenter the picture now.

CLEMMA. You lookin' for me to take care of you? I ain't the Lord's unemployment office, you know.

LEWIS. I'll find work. I always have.

CLEMMA. Cuttin' hair?

LEWIS. No. I gave up cuttin' hair because of this. (*He holds up his left hand. The fingers are gnarled and almost closed.*) Woke up one mornin' and the fingers went dead on me. Can't hold scissors in it and that's the one I had my talent in. I'm just learnin' to tie my shoes with one hand.

CLEMMA. Lewis, you are somethin', ain't you? . . . If you got any more things that have gone dead or ain't workin', tell me now and get it over with.

LEWIS. No. That's it. Except for my blind eye and my dead fingers, I'm healthy as a horse.

CLEMMA. A horse like that would have trouble findin' work too . . . (*She moves away from the table.*) No. It's too late, Lewis. Too late for me to ever get hurt like that again.

LEWIS. It wouldn't happen again, Clemma. I'm a changed man.

CLEMMA. (*Nods.*) I can see that from here, Lewis.

LEWIS. Well, you think about it. I have a friend I can stay with. He has a gas station up the road a few miles.

CLEMMA. I'd felt more wanted than needed if you'd come back here before all hell broke lose in you body.

LEWIS. I can still see what I want and I got the strength in my good hand to take care of both of us . . . You ponder it, Clemma. That's all I ask.

(*Disappointed,* Lewis *gets up, puts on his hat, picks up his bag, turns to go.*)

CLEMMA. You didn't eat your pie.

LEWIS. I'll take it with me, if you don't mind.

(*Lewis starts to put a napkin over it.*)

CLEMMA. (*She watches* Lewis, *then* . . .) Lewis! . . . I got a lotta extra work to do today. I guess I could use another hand around here.
LEWIS. (*Smiles, holds up his right hand.*) You mean like this one.

(Clemma *covers her face and laughs.*)

CLEMMA. Excuse me for laughin'.
LEWIS. That's more than I was hopin' for.
CLEMMA. You can stay till after dinner, if you want.
LEWIS. That's more than I was expectin'.
CLEMMA. I'll tell you this, Lewis. I'm puzzled. 'Cause I don' know who the Lord's lookin' after now. You . . . or me.

(*Their eyes meet.*)

From Act II, scene iii:
Sammii and Vinnie—20-25

Vinnie, a young gangster who fractures the language, met Josie while dancing with her in Miami. During their brief interlude, Josie imparted simple wisdom that enabled Vinnie to overcome a problem situation. Appreciating this, he has tracked her down to give her a token of his appreciation—an inscribed broach he crafted himself. At the gathering, when Vinnie met Sammii, a dim but gorgeous package, there was an immediate, mutual attraction.

Here, after returning from the woods, they are alone for the first time:

(*Vinnie is wearing an open necked sports shirt, a gold chain around his neck, blue and white shoes and a white suit. His dialect is very New York. Sammii is young and gorgeous in a model sort of way.*)

SAMMII. So what do you do?

VINNIE. I work part time for my Uncle Georgio. Biggest foreign car distributor in South Florida.

SAMMII. And what do you do the other part time?

VINNIE. (*Looks around.*) You won't laugh?

SAMMII. Cross my heart . . . What do you do?

VINNIE. I make my own jewelry . . . Not for sale. Just for friends, family. Sounds a little fruity, right?

SAMMII. No. I don't think it sounds fruity at all . . . What have you made?

VINNIE. (*Fingers chain around his neck.*) This gold chair . . . You notice the intricate detail? The links are intraceptable to the naked eye . . . Look close.

SAMMII. (*Leans in and looks.*) You're right. I can hardly see them.

VINNIE. You like this ring? A genuine Bavasi.

SAMMII. Incredible . . . Did you make the diamond too?

VINNIE. No, you can't make diamonds, you get them from a wholesaler . . . How about this watch? Swiss movement.

SAMMII. (*Taking no notice.*) You made *that?*

VINNIE. Just the outside. I need a Swiss guy for the movement.

(Sammii *looks at Vinnie in amazement. He leans over and kisses her mouth, then backs away.*)

SAMMII. So, what made you get interested in this?

VINNIE. Well, when I was a kid, we went to see my family in Italy. And one day we go to the Vatican. The place where the Pope lives.

SAMMII. Yes. I know.

VINNIE. And in all these glass cases, I see all these silver and gold crosses and these diamond encrusted sceptricals . . . Is that right?

SAMMII. Sceptricals? I'm not sure.

VINNIE. Kings hold 'em in their arms to let people know they're kings.

SAMMII. Skeptres, I think.

VINNIE. Oh. Skeptres. Right . . . Anyway, I get this catalogue. "Treasures of the Vatican" . . . And I see these pictures of the world's greatest treasures, works of unimaginable valuable-ness, and I say to myself, "Hey! I can do that." But what I wanna do, is make somethin' good enough to give to the Pope . . . from the People of South Flordia.

SAMMII. You are so special.

VINNIE. Now I know I'm not good enough yet. And I know if I make, what? Like a gold I.D. bracelet, the Pope ain't gonna wear it. 'Cause if he lost it, people already know where he lives, right?

SAMMII. (*Amused.*) Do they ever.

VINNIE. So I make all this stuff for practice. But one day, before I die, I'm gonna get a handwritten note from the Pope that says, "Dear Vinnie, Adomino, Adominus, and thank you, People of South Florida" . . . Crazy, heh?

SAMMII. No. Not at all. So where do you know Josie from?

VINNIE. Met her in Miami. Danced with her once. Took her for a walk. This is one smart girl, this Josie. She stopped me from doin' somethin' real stupid once.

SAMMII. What was that?

VINNIE. I was gonna fly up to New York, kidnap Buzzi, bring her back to Florida and lock her in my basement until she says yes.

SAMMII. You're joking?

VINNIE. No. So Josie turns to me and gives me one word of advise . . . One little word . . . She says, "Don't!" . . . I hardly knew the girl and she says to me, "Don't" . . . and I didn't. Because I trusted her.

SAMMII. That's an incredible story.

VINNIE. Now I just gotta get her alone for two minutes, 'cause I got this little present I made for her. (*He takes out a small jewelry box.*)

SAMMII. May I ask what?

VINNIE. A brewch. A solid gold brewch . . . that says, "Don't" . . . You think she'll like it?

SAMMII. What girl wouldn't?

VINNIE. You now you're easier to talk to than Buzzi. You involved with anyone?

SAMMII. Well, sort of. With Ray . . . I think he really wants to get serious . . . But I'm just not ready to get involved . . . especially with a writer . . . because they're thinkin' all the time . . . I like that you talk and that you never think.

VINNIE. Thank you.

SAMMII. I'm looking to break it off but I just don't know how to tell him without hurting him.

VINNIE. That's no problem. I'll tell him.

SAMMII. Oh, no.

VINNIE. (*Gets up, energized.*) Sure. It's more humane. Don't dangle a guy on a rod and reel. Cut the line or shoot him. Come on.

(*Vinnie pulls Sammii into the woods.*)

From Act II, scene iv:
Josie—20-25
Annie—45-50

Josie, at odds with her mother, resenting her for leaving her father, has just had a critical talk with Clemma during which Clemma gave sage advise, warning her of the soul-poisoning effects of harboring anger. Clemma further enlightened Josie to the fact her father, consumed with business, wasn't there for her when she was growing up but her mother was.

When Josie attempts to postpone a needed conversation with Annie, Annie will have none of it. It is time to clear the air.

ANNIE. Josie—

JOSIE. Mom, could—could we just skip it for tonight. I will do it, I promise. Tomorrow or the day after. Could we?

ANNIE. We can't keep putting it off forever, Josie. I can't deal one more minute with this—this hatred you have for me.

JOSIE. I don't hate you, Mother. I was angry before, yes. But I need something else right now that you can't give me.

ANNIE. What's that?

JOSIE. I'm not ready for him to go yet. I don't want this to be his last summer. I don't want to close up this house tonight and never be able to see him sitting in that chair, warming himself in the sun and thinking how great it once was. When we were a family.

ANNIE. Nobody can give you that, Josie.

JOSIE. I know that. And I will love you again. I promise. Do you think I could go through burying him without you to hold on to? But somehow this silly little child in me is still hoping for a happy ending. That you'll leave Walter and come back to Dad. And we'd all have one last summer again. It's not going to happen, I know that. But I don't have to know it tonight. Tonight. That's all I'm talking about.

ANNIE. I understand. I do. Oh, Josie. I just want to put my arms around you and make it alright. But I can't wait. I'll wait as long as you want, sweetheart.

JOSIE. (*Bursts into tears, throws arms around her mother.*) I love you. I really do, Mom. I just wish it would get better right away.

ANNIE. I know. I know, baby . . . Shh, it's alright. I'm here for you.

(Annie *and* Josie *hold each other.*)

About Neil Simon

Neil Simon was born in New York City, New York, in 1927 and graduated from New York University, 1946. He holds an Honorary Doctorate of Humane Letters from Hofstra University, 1981, and an Honorary Doctorate from Williams College, 1984. His plays are *Come Blow Your Horn, Little Me* (musical), *Barefoot in the Park, The Odd Couple, Sweet Charity* (musical) *The Star-Spangled Girl, Plaza Suite, Promises, Promises* (musical), *Last of the Red Hot Lovers, The Gingerbread Lady, The Prisoner of Second Avenue, The Sunshine Boys, The Good Doctor, God's Favorite, California Suite, Chapter Two, They're Playing Our Song, I Ought to Be in Pictures, Fools, Little Me, Brighton Beach Memoirs, Biloxi Blues, The Odd Couple* (female version), *Broadway Bound, Rumors, Lost in Yonkers, Jake's Women, The Goodbye Girl (musical), Laughter on the 23rd Floor, London Suite, Hotel Suite,* and *The Dinner Party.*

Neil Simon has also written extensively for television and motion pictures. His awards include the Pulitzer Prize for *Lost in Yonkers*; Emmy awards for the "Sid Caesar Show" and "The Phil Silvers Show"; Tony awards for *The Odd Couple, Biloxi Blues* (Best Play), and *Lost in Yonkers* (Best Play); Tony nominations for *Little Me, Barefoot in the Park, Plaza Suite, Last of the Red Hot Lovers, The Prisoner of Second Avenue, Brighton Beach Memoirs, Broadway Bound,* and *Promises, Promises.* Mr. Simon also holds the Writers Guild screen award for *The Odd Couple* and *The Out-of-Towners,* the Writers Guild Laurel Award, the Evening Standard Award, the Sam S. Shubert award, and the American Comedy Award for Lifetime Achievement. He received the Writers Guild Screen Award nominations for *Barefoot in the Park* and an Oscar nomination for *The Odd Couple.*

ORDER DIRECT

A WOMAN SPEAKS: WOMEN FAMOUS, INFAMOUS and UNKNOWN, ed. Cosentino. $12.95.
BETH HENLEY: MONOLOGUES for WOMEN, Henley. *Crimes of the Heart*, others. $8.95.
CLASSIC MOUTH, ed. Cosentino. Speeches for kids from famous literature. $8.95.
COLD READING and HOW to BE GOOD at IT, Hoffman. $12.95.
DIALECT MONOLOGUES, Karshner/Stern. Book and cassette tape. $19.95.
DIALECT MONOLOGUES, VOL. II, Karshner/Stern. Book and cassette tape. $19.95.
DIALECT MONOLOGUES—CD VERSION, Karshner/Stern. $22.95.
FITTING IN. Monologues for kids, Mauro. $8.95.
FOR WOMEN: MONOLOGUES THEY HAVEN'T HEARD, Pomerance. $9.95.
FOR WOMEN: MORE MONOS THEY HAVEN'T HEARD, Pomerance. $9.95.
FOR WOMEN: POCKET MONOLOGUES from SHAKESPEARE, Dotterer. $9.95.
HIGH-SCHOOL MONOLOGUES THEY HAVEN'T HEARD, Karshner. $9.95.
KIDS' STUFF, Roddy. 30 great audition pieces for children. $9.95.
KNAVES, KNIGHTS, and KINGS, ed. Dotterer. Shakespeare's speeches for men. $8.95.
MINUTE MONOLOGUES for KIDS, Roddy. $9.95.
MODERN MONOLOGUES for MODERN KIDS, Mauro. $9.95.
MODERN SCENES for WOMEN, Pomerance. Scenes for today's actresses. $7.95.
MONOLOGUES for KIDS, Roddy. 28 wonderful speeches for boys and girls. $9.95.
MONOLOGUES for TEENAGE GIRLS, Pomerance. $9.95.
MONOLOGUES for TEENAGERS, Karshner. Contemporary teen speeches. $9.95.
MONOLOGUES from CHEKHOV, trans. Cartwright. $8.95.
MONOLOGUES from GEORGE BERNARD SHAW, ed. Michaels. $7.95.
MONOLOGUES from MOLIERE, trans. Dotterer. $9.95.
MONOLOGUES from OSCAR WILDE, ed. Michaels. $7.95.
MONOLOGUES from the CLASSICS, ed. Karshner. $8.95.
MONOLOGUES THEY HAVEN'T HEARD, Karshner. Speeches for men and women. $9.95.
MORE MONOLOGUES HAVEN'T HEARD, Karshner. More living-language speeches. $9.95.
MORE MONOLOGUES for KIDS, Roddy. More great speeches for boys and girls. $9.95.
MORE MONOLOGUES for TEENAGERS, Karshner. $9.95.
NEIL SIMON MONOLOGUES, ed. Karshner. $14.95.
NEIL SIMON SCENES, ed. Karshner. $14.95.
POCKET MONOLOGUES for MEN, Karshner. $9.95.
POCKET MONOLOGUES for WOMEN, Pomerance. 30 modern speeches. $9.95.
POCKET MONOLOGUES: WORKING-CLASS CHARACTERS for WOMEN, Pomerance. $8.95.
RED LICORICE, Tippit. 31 great scene-monologues for preteens. $9.95.
SCENES for KIDS, Roddy. 30 scenes for girls and boys. $9.95.
SCENES for TEENAGERS, Karshner. Scenes for today's teen boys and girls. $9.95.
SHAKESPEARE'S LADIES, ed. Dotterer. $9.95.
SHAKESPEARE'S MONOLOGUES for WOMEN, ed. Dotterer. $9.95.
SHAKESPEARE'S MONOLOGUES THEY HAVEN'T HEARD, ed. Dotterer. $9.95.
TEENAGE MOUTH, Karshner. Modern monologues for young men and women. $9.95.
VOICES. Speeches from the writings of famous women, ed. Cosentino. $9.95.
WHEN KIDS ACHIEVE, Mauro. Positive monologues for preteen boys and girls. $8.95.
WOMAN, Pomerance. Monologues for actresses. $8.95.
YOU SAID a MOUTHFUL, Karshner. Tongue twisters galore. $8.95.

Visit our on-line catalog at: dramaline.com

Send your check or money order (no cash or COD) plus handling charges of $4.00 for the first book and $1.50 for each additional book. California residents add 8.25 % tax. Send your order to: Dramaline Publications, 36-851 Palm View Road, Rancho Mirage, California 92270-2417.